More praise for *Ready to Be a Thought Leader?*

"enise Brosseau's ground-breaking book teaches us how to make our careers natter, changing ourselves and others for the better. If you are ready to live your fe to its full potential, I highly recommend *Ready to Be a Thought Leader?*."

—Sheryle Bolton, CEO, Sally Ride Science, Inc.

"At 85 Broads, we help smart women develop the leadership skills they need to dramatically increase the lifetime return on the investment they make in their careers. To do that, they need to know how to build a network of dedicated followers around their game-changing ideas. *Ready to Be a Thought Leader?* is just the kind of savvy, inspirational, and engaging guide to help anyone break out of the pack and stand out for all the right reasons."

—Janet Hanson, founder, 85 Broads

"As a long-time technology executive who has experienced several career transitions, I have learned the importance of thought leadership to raise my own profile within the industry and open the door to new opportunities for myself and others. *Ready to Be a Thought Leader?* offers just the sort of practical advice that I could have used along the way. I highly recommend this book for every executive."

—Beth Devin, chief information officer, Silicon Valley Bank

"To climb the corporate ladder, you not only have to know where you are going, but you have to bring people along with you. Denise Brosseau teaches you how to enhance your credibility and find encouragement from a broad constituency supporting you."

—Lydia I. Beebe, corporate secretary and chief governance officer,
Chevron Corporation

"Whether you're an entrepreneur, an executive, or running a nonprofit, *Ready to Be a Thought Leader?* will help you establish your credibility within and outside your organization and create a tribe of dedicated followers."

—Sheryl O'Loughlin, executive director, Center of Entrepreneurial Studies,
Graduate School of Business, Stanford University; cofounder and former
CEO, Plum, Inc.; and former CEO, Clif Bar and Company

"As the CEO of a large nonprofit, I know the importance of finding and engaging with a passionate set of people who believe in and will engage with our work, and one way for me to do that is by establishing myself as a thought leader. *Ready to Be a Thought Leader?* provides the strategies and resources entrepreneurs need to have their ideas not only heard, but acted on. I recommend it as a must-read."

—Telle Whitney, president and CEO, Anita Borg Institute

"*Ready to Be a Thought Leader?* provides tips, tools, and resources that will
you articulate your passion, demonstrate your leadership, and engage other
accelerating new and creative initiatives. Denise provides a step-by-step proc
to gain strategic visibility for your ideas and your work and in turn the v
contribution you make to improving the world. A must-read for anyone w
wants to be more strategic and systematic in their work as a change agent."

— Ellen Snee, EdD, vice president, leadership programs, VMwa

"Is it time to stand out from the crowd and gain more recognition for your achiev
ments? *Ready to Be a Thought Leader?* will open your eyes to new possibilitie
for increasing your visibility and credibility within any organization — just wha
every savvy executive needs to get ahead."

— Miranda Lin, senior vice president, Bank of America

"To rise above the noise, you need to stand out as a trusted and reliable resource for
your customers. Denise Brosseau's timely and engaging new book, *Ready to Be
a Thought Leader?*, shows just what it takes for executives and CEOs to become
that go-to guru. Her strategies will ensure that customers flock to your door."

— Mike Gill, vice president, US Sales and Customer Care,
Medtronic Diabetes

"As a Silicon Valley executive talent agent, Denise Brosseau has a front-row seat on
what it really takes to stand out from the crowd. In *Ready to Be a Thought Leader?*,
she shares that know-how in an easy-to-read, down-to-earth, and approachable
style."

— Kit Yarrow, consumer psychologist; coauthor, *Gen BuY*; and professor,
Golden Gate University

"Whether you're an up-and-coming entrepreneur or an established executive,
Denise Brosseau will provide you specific guidance and invaluable insights to
help you take control of your business and career. Denise's stories, examples,
templates, and tools have — to quote one of her case studies — the 'strong smell of
reality.' She's been there, done that, and helped hundreds of clients get to where
you want to go."

— David Newman, author, *Do It! Marketing*

"If you're ready to break out as the 'go-to' person in your niche, *Ready to Be
a Thought Leader?* will cut ten years off your learning curve. With actionable
advice, a step-by-step execution plan, and inspirational stories of leaders, this
book will help you put your career on overdrive!"

— Dan Schawbel, author, *Me 2.0* and *Promote Yourself*

READY TO BE A THOUGHT LEADER?

READY TO BE A THOUGHT LEADER?

How to Increase Your Influence, Impact, and Success

DENISE BROSSEAU

JB JOSSEY-BASS™

A Wiley Brand

Published by Jossey-Bass
A Wiley Brand
One Montgomery Street, Suite 1200, San Francisco, CA
94104-4594—www.josseybass.com

Jossey-Bass books and products are available through most bookstores. To contact Jossey-Bass directly call our Customer Care Department within the U.S. at 800-956-7739, outside the U.S. at 317-572-3986, or fax 317-572-4002.

Wiley publishes in a variety of print and electronic formats and by print-on-demand. Some material included with standard print versions of this book may not be included in e-books or in print-on-demand. If this book refers to media such as a CD or DVD that is not included in the version you purchased, you may download this material at http://booksupport.wiley.com. For more information about Wiley products, visit www.wiley.com.

Library of Congress Cataloging-in-Publication Data

Brosseau, Denise, 1959-
  Ready to be a thought leader : how to increase your influence, impact, and success / Denise Brosseau.—First edition.
     1 online resource.
  Includes index.
    ISBN 978-1-118-79506-4 (pdf)—ISBN 978-1-118-79511-8 (epub)—
ISBN 978-1-118-64761-5 (hardback) 1. Leadership. 2. Creative thinking. 3. Thought and thinking. 4. Organizational change. I. Title.
  HD57.7
  658.4'092—dc23
                                                                        2013039255

Printed in the United States of America
FIRST EDITION
HB Printing 10 9 8 7 6 5 4 3 2 1

I dedicate this book to my mother and my mastermind team.
Without them this book would not have been possible.

CONTENTS

FOREWORD
GUY KAWASAKI

People use the term "thought leader" as if all you have to do to become one is set up a Twitter account and start tweeting. This is hardly the case. True thought leaders have expertise, passion, and a track record of changing the world. They become thought leaders when they rise above themselves by sharing their knowledge so that others can change the world, too. Perhaps most importantly, they are recognized by their peers—they do not declare themselves. It is only through a sincere commitment to share the path forward to a better future that they earn the right to be called a thought leader.

Achieving the status of thought leader—while it will not happen overnight—is absolutely worth the effort. You'll gain a seat at the table and the credibility you need to build a more successful company or catapult your career to the next level.

If you want to know how to become this kind of go-to guy or gal in your industry, community, or profession, I suggest that you read this book. Denise Brosseau explains just what it takes to achieve this lofty status. If you have a world-changing idea with the potential to make a real difference, she'll show you the steps to take to get recognized and respected for the work you've done, and how to get others to adopt and evangelize on behalf of that big idea.

I first met Denise in 1998 when I was starting Garage.com. I invited her and her team at the Forum for Women Entrepreneurs to camp out in our offices because I observed that Denise was just as committed as I was to helping start-up companies succeed. Since then, Denise has helped hundreds of entrepreneurs and executives build bigger businesses and more successful careers as the cofounder of the Springboard Venture Forums, the Invent Your Future Conference, and the founder of Thought Leadership Lab. She has also become a respected voice and go-to expert in leadership and entrepreneurship, becoming a true thought leader herself in the process.

If you're ready to break out of the pack, read this book—not for just yourself but for your team and for anyone else that you can inspire.

Guy Kawasaki is a special advisor to the Motorola business unit of Google. He is also the author of *APE, What the Plus!*, *Enchantment*, and nine other books. Previously, he was the chief evangelist of Apple. Kawasaki has a BA from Stanford University and an MBA from UCLA, as well as an honorary doctorate from Babson College.

INTRODUCTION
WHAT DO YOU WANT TO BE KNOWN FOR?

The first time she called me for some career advice, Van Ton-Quinlivan was finishing a one-year stint as the chief of staff to the chairman of one of the largest utilities in the United States. As we sat down that weekend at the kitchen table in her Bay Area home, Van laid out a few professional options she was considering. We agreed that one of them clearly gave her an opportunity to make a lasting impact in an arena that really mattered to her: workforce development.

That afternoon we created a detailed plan, and over the next four years I served as Van's advisor and sounding board as she advanced from being the founding director of workforce development at her company to testifying in front of the U.S. Senate on workforce issues. This was followed by recognition from the White House for her company's best practices in workforce development, and then by an appointment from the governor of California to oversee workforce development and career technical education for the state's community college system—one of the largest in the world.

Along the way, Van went from being completely unknown in the workforce development world to becoming a recognized thought leader who impacts legislation; serves on national boards, committees, and commissions; and has been quoted at length by Thomas Friedman in his Sunday column in the *New York Times*. Her programs have been replicated; she has promulgated concepts that have become industry norms; and now—harkening back to that old E. F. Hutton commercial—when Van talks, people listen.

Today I have the privilege of advising lots of leaders like Van—including start-up CEOs and Fortune 500 executives—on how to make their own transition from leader to thought leader. At Thought Leadership Lab we work with clients who want to be more successful but not only as measured by the dollars in their bank accounts. Our role is to push them to think beyond their wallets to the *influence* they can wield for positive change, the *impact* they can have in arenas that matter to them, and the *legacy* they can leave behind after they move on.

WHAT IS A THOUGHT LEADER?

Do you want to become someone who can move and inspire others with your innovative ideas, turn those ideas into reality, and then create a dedicated group of friends, fans, and followers to help you replicate and scale those ideas into sustainable change?

This is the work of a thought leader.

Some thought leaders start an initiative, program, company, or movement. Others convene or lead an advisory committee, task force, or industry professional association. Some develop a product, platform, service, or training model. Others push for new legislation or modifications to existing regulations. Many create or put into practice their own framework or methodology and share it widely.

Regardless of the form of their engagement, they do not simply pontificate on what needs to be done; they actively engage in bringing to life new, first-of-their-kind projects, programs, and creative initiatives. It is those actions that influence and inspire others to get on board.

Getting others on board is critical. A thought leader is defined by her or his ability to galvanize others to think new thoughts, modify the way they have always done things, and embark on new behaviors, new paths, and new actions to transform the world.

Thought leaders are all around us. In Boston, Robin Chase, the cofounder of the car-sharing company Zipcar, has built on her credibility from that role to encourage audiences of thousands to think about how their individual actions can have a direct impact on global climate change.[1] In Chicago, Nina Nashif, the founder of the start-up incubator Healthbox, is building a platform as a healthcare innovator—speaking and blogging and writing her first book.[2] And in Los Angeles, there's artist and designer Ron Finley, the cofounder of the charity L.A. Green Grounds, who styles himself as the "Gangsta Gardener" in order to encourage Angelenos to cultivate vegetable and fruit gardens in vacant lots within deprived neighborhoods.[3]

In big towns and small, you will find attorneys, executives, consultants, bankers, social entrepreneurs, and people from every walk of life who have stepped into the role of thought leader in order to move their agenda forward.

I admire thought leaders like Robin and Nina and Ron, who change the world in meaningful ways and engage others to join their efforts. They create evolutionary and even revolutionary advancements in their fields, not just by urging others to be open to new ways of thinking but when they create a blueprint for people to follow—a method, process, guidelines, or a set of best practices. Thought leaders who codify the steps necessary for following in their path assure that others will align with and build on their success. This guarantees that they, as leaders, are not confined to making small tweaks around the edges but instead create a foundation for others to build on or a movement for others to join.

WHY BECOME A THOUGHT LEADER?

This is all well and good, you might be thinking. But why should I make the transition from leader to thought leader?

What I have witnessed over and over is that thought leadership is the key that unlocks a whole new level of professional accomplishment and achievement as well as career and personal satisfaction.

If you'd like to increase your *strategic visibility*—by which I mean your visibility and standing with the people who matter—then thought leadership is one of the easiest paths to achieve that. I've seen thought leaders become *rainmakers* who attract customers for their products, clients for their services, partners for their companies, followership for their blogs, readership for their books, and funders for projects they have under way.

Thought leadership leads to *exposure for your ideas* both inside and outside your company, particularly with journalists, analysts, event organizers, and conference hosts. It will give you *access* to people who can help you *make things happen*—leaders in your organization or community; innovators in your profession or industry; or influencers in government or regulatory circles.

As a recognized thought leader you will have the *power* to persuade, the *status and authority* to move things in a new direction, and the *clout* to implement real progress and widespread innovation. People want to affiliate with those who are well known and in the know. Thus, thought leadership also leads to invitations to join corporate boards, serve on government commissions, and participate in industry-wide committees—opportunities to *raise your profile* from the local to the national to the international stage.

Thought leadership is not about being known; it is about being known *for making a difference.* A thought leader is seen as a *credible, reliable authority,* an "honest broker," someone whom others can safely look to for guidance, valuable insights, and a plan for what to do next. That credibility is essentially based on *trust,* trust that you, as a thought leader, know (or will find) a way to do things better, cheaper, faster, or more efficiently. Trust that you will help people solve their problems, their community's problems, or the intractable problems faced by their friends and families. Trust that you will take the risk to put your ideas and opinions forward, to speak out even when you might be wrong (and correct yourself when you are), to be a *role model* and set an example by your actions, which others can emulate.

Yes, to become a recognized and respected thought leader takes time—usually several years—and there are some risks: you will be in the spotlight, which means you may take some pretty painful arrows. But being in the spotlight can also bring about a *promotion* or a better job, an *award* or an unexpected accolade, a portrait on the cover of the *Wall Street Journal* or a story in an industry magazine that engages your community to finally unite around the fundamental transformation you have been advocating. More likely than not, it will lead to an *unexpected invitation* to open a new door to an opportunity that you never thought was possible, including the chance to encourage and support others to become thought leaders in their own right.

And perhaps most importantly, for many it can answer the deeper questions: Why am I here? What is the meaning in my work? What will I leave behind? As your influence and platform grow, so will your opportunities to *create a significant impact* on a larger and larger scale, to *inspire* and bring about *meaningful change* that can last long after you're gone. As a thought leader, you will *leave a lasting legacy*: transformed teams, communities, industries, systems, or governments.

Obviously, not everyone chooses to be a thought leader—to put themselves out in front of their field. Most follow the traditional career advice we were all taught was the path to success: keep your head down, work hard, and take each step, one by one, up the ladder. If you're lucky, and I hope you are, this route will routinely pay off for you with promotions, salary raises, and job security.

But that's not always the case, is it? What I've witnessed all too frequently (especially through the economic downturns that seem to follow one after another) is that if you take the traditional route, there comes a point in time when things no longer go your way. Your champion retires or leaves the company; your company is sold or merged; or your industry moves off in an entirely new direction.

Technologies evolve, funding dries up, or customers revise their preferences overnight. Your path to the next job, to a partnership position, or to full tenure is blocked; your party is now out of power or your boss falls out of favor.

The result? That long sought-after career goal, the one you may have worked towards for years, may no longer be attainable or anywhere near as desirable.

The good news? *Thought leadership is the very best career insurance around.*

As the best-connected, most-respected, and most highly valued people in their organizations or industries, thought leaders, I've found, are usually the last to find themselves without a role or opportunity when things go awry. Their supporters and followers often become their allies, able to help them identify new paths forward after an unexpected company acquisition, reorganization, or downturn. Their wide network of connections, communities, and constituencies makes them much more likely to find the next place to land without any significant difficulty or detour along the way.

THOUGHT LEADERS NEEDED

The fact is that the world needs a lot more people who will step beyond traditional leadership roles into the role of thought leader.

One person who understands this is Katie Orenstein, CEO of the OpEd Project. Her organization offers programs in companies, universities, and in public settings, which teach people to think about what they know, why it matters, and how they can use their knowledge and expertise to change the world. She believes that "thought leadership is like citizenship, that having a voice is like having a vote—having a say in what goes on in the world."[4] I couldn't agree more. I am on a mission to encourage everyone to add their voice to the conversation in their community, industry, and at the national level. More people with an informed point of view speaking up and speaking out will make a difference for us all.

Another perspective comes from Erika Brown Ekiel, former *Forbes* journalist and founder of Storyboard, a company that helps individual thought leaders get their stories out into the world. Erika has found that "people don't care what companies do, they care what leaders do." She advises her clients, "Editors are no longer the arbiters of what is genius or cool or worth hearing. But, on the other side of the coin, with fewer journalists spending less time on any individual story, editors also need more content. They need content particularly from credible sources. This provides a win-win for thought leaders with a unique story to tell."[5]

So why aren't more people stepping up to thought leadership?

In five years of working with aspiring thought leaders, I've found that what often stops people is inside their own heads—what one of my clients calls the "itty bitty shitty committee," those negative voices that tell us we can't possibly achieve our dreams or that no one wants to hear what we have to say. I admit I have them too, and sometimes they can be *very* loud. So we procrastinate, find myriad excuses, or create distractions that hold us back, instead of surrounding ourselves with allies and supporters who can help us make our dreams a reality.

Throughout the book, we'll look at what to do when you get stopped and explore how to overcome the roadblocks you might encounter (personal responsibilities, a difficult boss, your age, your background, even your reticence to take center stage). We'll talk about how to build new skills, form new attitudes, and find a new path when naysayers, credit-stealers, or backbiters block the first (because sadly those folks *are* out there).

The path to thought leadership is not always easy—I wish I could say it was—but it is possible. *And it is important.*

The key is to realize how important. Whatever issue you are tackling, whatever problem you are working to solve, whatever arena you choose to educate and inspire and engage others in—it needs *your* voice. To stay on the sidelines or keep silent or not value your own participation will mean not only that you will lose the opportunity to make a difference but that the rest of us will lose too. We will lose your passion, your commitment, and your dedication to making a difference. We will lose your good ideas and your vision of a better future. We will lose your unique story and your ability to have a meaningful impact on the issues you care about.

I want to empower and equip more people to become thought leaders, including executives, entrepreneurs, service professionals, and community leaders. I also want to inspire those who are traditionally overlooked—by the mainstream media, by the leaders of corporations mired in old thinking, and by elected officials—to believe that their voices do, indeed, matter. I believe we need more people who have the skills and motivation to create a clear direction, goal, and meaningful plan of action—people who are ready to create, and help the world create, evolutionary and revolutionary change more quickly, intentionally, and effectively. That's why I wrote this book.

When I began my own evolution from leader to thought leader, I could have used a book like this, a simple how-to guide that would help me find my way and motivate me to keep going.

MY JOURNEY TO THOUGHT LEADERSHIP

Let me tell you a little bit about my own thought leadership journey. In three years, from 1998 through early 2001, I went from being a relatively unknown leader of a small nonprofit in Silicon Valley to being quoted in the *New York Times*, recognized as one of the Top 25 Women on the Web, feted as a Woman of Influence, and featured in *Inc. Magazine*, *Fast Company*, and on the cover of the technology industry magazine *Upside*. I was invited to share my ideas at major universities; to speak at local, national, and even international conferences; and to participate at the White House in coalitions to advance women's entrepreneurship nationally.

During that time, the organization I cofounded, the Forum for Women Entrepreneurs, expanded from one city to seven, and investors, associations, and prestigious foundations began to seek us out, eager to replicate our model nationwide and offering collaboration and funding. This allowed us to expand our membership from 250 to 1,200 and to grow our budget to be among the top 5 percent of nonprofits in the United States. In 1999, I also had the opportunity to cofound Springboard, the first venture conference for women entrepreneurs, which has since led to over $6 billion (and counting!) in increased investment in women-founded and women-led businesses.[6]

And then, in the spring of 2001, the heady whirlwind all came to a screeching halt, virtually overnight.

The dot-com crash brought an end to the hot IPO market and the funding frenzy that not only had allowed so many women entrepreneurs for the first time to secure venture funding for their companies, but had also allowed an executive from a small nonprofit to unexpectedly gain the national spotlight. Instead of seventy-five new members signing up to join our organization every month, the phones were all but silent. Instead of people clamoring to be a part of every event we hosted, we were struggling to fill even small event venues. And our bank account quickly went from flush to fumes as our sponsors—the major banks, accounting firms, and law firms who had supported us—ran for cover.

There had been little warning, although looking back, I suppose I should have known it couldn't last. But no one wants to think that way when they have the opportunity to take an all-expenses-paid trip to be one of the judges for the first international business-plan contest in Scotland. When the press is calling you regularly, you have a book deal on the table, and you're the first person in your extended family to get invited to the White House, you want to hold on tight and hope it lasts forever.

But it doesn't. At least it didn't for me.

That's another reason I wrote this book. When I look back, could I have predicted my meteoric rise from obscurity to national prominence? Never. Could I have enjoyed it more? I'm not sure.

Could I have been better prepared and done more to leverage my newfound celebrity in order to have a bigger impact in my niche and expand my access to the next job or opportunity? To that question I would answer a very resounding *yes*. And that's why I do what I do today.

After I left the nonprofit world, I started an executive talent agency in Silicon Valley, which I now call Thought Leadership Lab. Running the Lab gives me a unique window on the world. My clients are start-up CEOs and executives of some of the largest and best-known companies, organizations, academic institutions, and nonprofits in the world. By most any measure, they have achieved a lot of success in their lives. But when I first meet them at cocktail parties, conferences, or while serving together on a board, they tell me the same thing: "I'm not 'there' yet. I want more."

They describe what they want as a promotion, more clients, or better pay. Sometimes they seek a new (and better) job. Sometimes they want to get the word out about what they are doing, to bring more attention to the efforts they have under way. But what I hear, underlying their words, is "I want more recognition, I want more influence, I want to have a bigger impact on the world—and I don't know how to go to the next level."

That's where I come in.

At Thought Leadership Lab, we help our clients figure out all the essential elements for success—like personal brand, how to identify their niche, and how to craft their key messages. We help them think through how to align and engage their stakeholders and sponsors and how to get on the right boards, committees, or commissions so that they can make a difference. We help them to define a process, system, or methodology they can call their own and identify the opportunities that will get the word out about their expertise.

What I love about this work is the opportunity to serve as a sounding board, to cheer my clients' successes, and warn them of potential obstacles ahead. My clients amaze me with their unique ways of seeing the world; as we craft a strategic plan and strategize how to overcome setbacks, we move their ideas from the sidelines into the mainstream conversation. As they become better known, we figure out how to parlay their newfound "fame" into opportunities to have an ever greater impact—in their niche and in the world. It is meaningful and rewarding work, and I feel lucky every day to do what I do.

SEVEN STEPS TO THOUGHT LEADERSHIP

Over the years, I have developed a time-tested, seven-step process to help individuals successfully transition from leader to thought leader. In this book, I will share that process with you. If you follow this step-by-step guide through the chapters, you'll learn how to bring your own ideas to the world, have an impact on an issue you care about, and leave a meaningful legacy of which you can be proud. Here's what it takes:

Step 1: Find Your Driving Passion

Thought leadership starts with focus and passion. You will be far more effective if you identify the one arena where your interests, expertise, credibility, and commitment align—your "thought leadership intersection point." Next you will craft a clear *What If?* future, a possible future that you are committed to bring about. When you identify and align to key trends, you will gain momentum and be well on your way to make a significant difference, not only in your company or community but across your industry or niche.

Step 2: Build Your Ripples of Influence

To build your first ripples of change, you'll test your ideas and opinions (often not yet fully baked) with knowledgeable stakeholders—colleagues, mentors, and friends—gather their input, and continually refine your thinking. By listening to what resonates, you will distill many different points of view into the kernel of a transformative idea that will bring about the *What If?*

future you envision. Those conversations will also inform you how to position and leverage your message to tell a bigger story that gets your first followers on board.

Step 3: Activate Your Advocates

To expand your influence beyond your existing team or organization will require that you attract supporters and well-connected advocates—community leaders, industry spokespeople, analysts, journalists, research groups, or national partners—who can champion your product, program, initiative, or idea to a much broader set of audiences. In this chapter, you'll learn to articulate what's in it for them and to create real momentum for change as well as how to move your message out of the reach of naysayers, the people determined to stop any transformation in its tracks.

Step 4: Put Your "I" on the Line

To build sustainable momentum for a new idea requires someone to show the way, someone willing to step into the limelight and say "follow me." We'll explore how you can "put your 'I' on the line"—overcoming any self-imposed limits to standing front and center and risking your reputation to espouse a new direction or vision of the future, often long before others agree with your point of view.

Step 5: Codify Your Lessons Learned

The essential difference between leaders and thought leaders is often the latter's ability to distill their know-how into a replicable model so that others can be inspired and empowered to expand on what those leaders have accomplished. This chapter will give you the tools to codify, test, and refine a repeatable and scalable blueprint for others who want to follow in your footsteps.

Step 6: Put Yourself on S.H.O.U.T.

To increase your credibility, strategic visibility, and reputation and gain recognition as a thought leader, you will have to get the word out about your activities, efforts, and lessons learned. You're not a thought leader if no one knows anything about you or what you've accomplished. You need to be "discoverable" and connect with those who can build on your ideas.

Step 7: Incite (R)Evolution

Has the transformation you've envisioned and worked towards begun to take hold? In this chapter, you'll learn to audit your progress to ensure that you gain traction for your ideas locally, regionally, nationally, and even internationally. As you accelerate and amplify your voice, you'll increase your influence, expand your impact, and build a sustainable community of followers that will carry forward your efforts. Here we'll also explore how to prevent burnout as you bring about the evolutionary and even revolutionary change that will be your legacy.

HOW TO USE THIS BOOK

In Chapters One through Three, you'll learn to build your own thought leadership platform around an idea. In Chapter Five, we'll discuss how to create a blueprint so others can join and replicate your efforts. Then, in Chapter Six, we'll explore how to get out and "S.H.O.U.T." widely about what you're up to, and finally, in Chapter Seven, we'll cover how to create a community that can continue your work. If you've already been on this adventure a while, you don't need to start at the very beginning of the book. Jump to Chapter Five or Six to find some tools and techniques that will accelerate your efforts. If you've hit a roadblock, turn to Chapter Four to discover some suggestions from other thought leaders on how to move forward. If the journey's a new one for you, I invite you to follow the playbook from start to finish.

Throughout the book, you'll find lots of tips, shortcuts, and encouragement. You'll also meet some amazing people who are changing the world. I've included these case studies to offer inspiration and new ideas for how to begin or jump-start your own thought leadership journey. The following chapter, "Getting Started," includes an assessment for evaluating your progress to date; we'll also explore the behaviors and characteristics of successful thought leaders. Throughout the book, too, you'll find exercises and resources at each stage of the process. You can also find more information, case studies, and resources at www.thought leadershiplab.com.

One quick aside: as I wrote this book, I learned that some people are not comfortable with the term *thought leader*. There is no question that this term has been misused or misapplied by self-proclaimed experts who are all about self-promotion (or simply personal wealth). But we needn't reject the phrase altogether. Instead, I advocate that we reclaim "thought leader" to denote the following: change agents whose intentions and efforts are aligned to improve the world and who then choose to have a more significant impact by sharing their expertise, knowledge, and lessons learned with others, aligning their efforts in a way that creates momentum for sustainable evolutionary and revolutionary change.

Those are the folks I am talking to in this book.

Those who are not satisfied with the status quo; those who are actively working to bring about needed improvements in their company or industry, in their region or field of expertise, in laws and attitudes and in the way things have always been done. I hope you are one of those people.

If you picked up this book because you've been asked to establish your company's thought leadership within your industry or you're part of a group that wants to develop a shared thought leadership platform, you too will find that the ideas in this book will be applicable to your efforts. If you aren't looking to gain the designation "thought leader" but you know that pursuing thought leadership strategies will help you get ahead in your career, establish your credibility in your community, or help you build your business, you'll also find a lot of ideas here.

Or perhaps you're mentoring or sponsoring someone and hope to inspire him or her to step into a broader role as a thought leader. You'll discover here lots of techniques and resources you can share and many ways to offer support and ultimately ensure the person's success.

And if you've already started on your own path to thought leadership, but you've hit a seemingly immovable roadblock, or if you are tired, discouraged, or almost burned out, you'll find any number of workarounds, some new directions, and a lot of the necessary motivation to keep moving forward.

THE TIME IS NOW

Hopefully, the idea of thought leadership inspires, motivates, and excites you and you don't think, "I could never do that."

You can.

Thought leaders do not have a special gene, any inborn talents, or a secret decoder ring. They exist in every industry, nation, and arena; they are men and women, young and old, and they come from every ethnic, cultural, and socioeconomic background.

They are not always confident—they have their moments of doubt. They are not always the smartest kid in the room; most will admit that even if they are the "expert" in their community, they still have a lot to learn and they have made (many) mistakes along the way. I know I have. And thought leaders do not always start out with a clear path, plan, or purpose. They have stumbled around, lost their way, and then, somehow, found it again.

And so will you.

If you crave more visibility for what you are already doing, read this book. If you want to build more credibility in order to advance an agenda or a big idea, read this book. If you are ready to use your skills and talents—and develop new ones—in order to make an indelible imprint on the world, then this book is for you.

And most importantly, if you want to leave a legacy that extends beyond a series of job titles on a resume, *please* read this book. I wrote it for you. I believe we need many more voices at the table, many more solutions proposed, and many more people inspired and empowered to build a purposeful life that serves and calls others to action.

Now is exactly the right time to begin your thought leadership journey.

Ready?

READY TO BE A THOUGHT LEADER?

GETTING STARTED
FROM LEADER
TO
THOUGHT LEADER

Are you ready to be the "go to" leader in your community or industry, to wield influence for positive change, have an impact in arenas that matter to you, and leave a legacy of consequence? Then you're probably eager to get started on your journey from leader to thought leader. But before we jump into the how-to details of each of the seven steps, let's see how far you've progressed to date.

Thought leadership is made up of a lot of different building blocks; you may find you've already made considerable headway in some areas, while in others you are just beginning. Below is an assessment matched with each of the steps and chapters in the book; it will give you a baseline of where you stand today as well as an overview of what you'll be learning in each step. After the assessment, we'll take a look at some of the common characteristics and behaviors of thought leaders.

HOW AM I DOING SO FAR?

Check off the items that you have completed or "mastered" so far. If you prefer to give yourself a score, count 1 point for each check—the maximum is 30 points.

Chapter 1: Find Your Driving Passion

✓ I can clearly define my thought leadership niche—where I want to be the recognized "go to" person.

✓ I have a clear view of the future that I'd like to see and bring about.

✓ I focus on big ideas that inspire and engage others.

✓ I understand the key trends in my industry or field and align my efforts with those trends.

Chapter 2: Build Your Ripples of Influence

✓ I am able to distill my knowledge, know-how, or past experiences into the kernel of a transformative idea.

✓ I test my thinking regularly, even newly hatched ideas, in order to find and build even bigger possibilities.

✓ I have a loyal group of friends, colleagues, or coworkers, past and present, that can and will help me test and implement a new project or initiative.

✓ I participate in many forums where I can exchange ideas with a wide variety of people inside and outside my organization; I regularly listen to others' points of view and lessons learned and integrate them with my own.

Chapter 3: Activate Your Advocates

✓ I have built a program, project, product, or initiative that has the potential to scale beyond what I can do on my own.

✓ I enjoy and have the skills to enroll others to adopt my vision of the future and join my team.

✓ I understand how to build incremental engagement—to not just bring people on board but get them to advocate my position.

✓ I have many well-known and well-respected advocates willing to champion my point of view broadly, and I am effective at activating them.

Chapter 4: Put Your "I" On the Line

✓ I believe my ideas are worth sharing.

✓ I am comfortable stepping into the limelight; I'm not afraid to speak up and share what I know in public forums (in person and online).

✓ I will risk my reputation, if necessary, to move my ideas or the needs of the community I stand for forward.

✓ I have put in place support structures to help me move forward despite any naysayers, credit-stealers, and personal challenges that may arise.

Chapter 5: Codify Your Lessons Learned

✓ I have distilled my experiences and crafted them as universal life lessons that can inform, inspire, and catalyze others to take action.

✓ I have developed a blueprint, methodology, or framework that others can follow to replicate what I have achieved.

✓ I have measurable, actionable, and verifiable evidence that proves my ideas are valid and can be replicated.

✓ I have tested, iterated, and packaged my blueprint into intellectual property that assures its successful replication.

✓ I have protected my intellectual property with licenses, trademarks, copyrights, or other safeguards in order to maintain the integrity of what's been created.

Chapter 6: Put Yourself on S.H.O.U.T.

✓ I have honed my writing and speaking skills so that people want to listen to and get on board with what I have under way.

✓ I have followers that I communicate with regularly (email, newsletter, Twitter, Facebook) to share resources and lessons learned in order to scale my efforts and initiatives.

(continued)

✓ I think about and manage my personal and social brand and guarantee that I am "discoverable."

✓ I have a book, white paper, talk, blog, or website where my ideas are codified and through which I inspire others to get on board.

✓ I attend or convene meetings, roundtables, or conferences, and I speak and network with potential clients, customers, and even critics.

Chapter 7: Incite (R)Evolution

✓ I regularly audit my impact to see who is commenting, forwarding, retweeting, or adopting my point of view.

✓ I see evolutionary and even revolutionary transformation that has come about as a result of my efforts and those of my followers.

✓ I have identified ways to pass the baton to fans and followers (books, licensed programs, train the trainers, legislation, or regulations).

✓ I regularly rest and renew to ensure that I don't burn out.

How are you doing? If you're ready to jump in and get started, then skip ahead. I won't be insulted. I'm impatient, too. Find the section with the building block you are focused on right now and start there. If you're new to the journey, don't get discouraged if you only have a few items you can check off on this list—that's why you're reading this book. If you've already completed every one of the thirty items, I hope you'll visit our Thought Leadership Lab Facebook page and share your story. (Actually, everyone is welcome to join our Facebook page! Please come visit.) Then perhaps it's time to think of an even bigger future you'd like to make possible and start again. If not, pass this book along to one of your followers to guarantee that they'll be empowered to carry on your work.

Now let's explore the shared characteristics and behaviors of thought leaders.

WHAT MAKES A SUCCESSFUL THOUGHT LEADER?

In many ways thought leaders are exactly like everyone else. In other ways they are pretty unique. Those that stand out tend to share a common set of characteristics: they expand ideas, they tell stories, they nurture long-lasting relationships, and they adopt behaviors that increase their momentum.

Thought Leaders Expand Ideas

Ideas are the bread and butter of thought leadership. At the core of every project, product, cause, or movement there is an idea—an idea that is meant to inspire new ways of thinking and engage action. Ideas form the core of what it means to change the world. People hire and promote thought leaders because they are "ideators" (defined by the Urban Dictionary as "a person who creates productive ideas"). In order to engage people with our ideas, we must nurture relentless curiosity, find and engage with our broader ecosystem, and show others the way forward. *What will you do this year to expand your ideas?*

Nurture Relentless Curiosity   Tom Kelley, the general manager of IDEO, one of the world's leading design firms, and author of *The Ten Faces of Innovation*, advocates that individuals and organizations constantly gather new sources of information in order to expand their knowledge and grow.[1] Don't wait around for inspiration to strike. Nurture relentless curiosity; continually explore and expand new possibilities. Question the status quo and ask, What might be the "next big thing"? Seek out novel ways of looking at the world, out-of-the-box solutions, and the sparks of innovation everywhere—in books, online, in meetings, at events.

How can you continuously expand your thinking? Look for great methodologies, processes, or innovative practices in other industries that you can bring to your own. Adopt and adapt the projects, programs, or initiatives of leaders from other regions.

Focus on implementing a new idea or modify one developed a hundred years ago. Regardless of the source, you can become the evangelist for a new way of thinking. Consistently refresh your point of view about the issues of the day in your industry or niche. *What new ideas and possibilities are you curious about?*

Engage with Your Ecosystem   Dan Gillmor, the director of the Walter Cronkite School of Journalism at Arizona State University, started his career as a journalist, most notably at the *San Jose Mercury News*. When he started writing his first column, he says, "Lots of people sent me email, mostly to tell me what I was missing, and what an idiot I was, but the 'what I was missing' was the really good stuff." He learned early a guiding principle that became the underpinning of everything he did: "My readers knew much more than I do. And from that, a conversation emerged."[2]

Seek out creative suggestions from, and collaborate with, those tackling the same challenges you are. Create a dialogue so that everyone's solutions and questions are heard, and valued. You don't need to know everything (or even have an amazing innovation of your own) before you begin. No one can possibly know everything; that's not the point.

The point is to find the broader ecosystem that cares about what you care about and then enter or create the conversation. The community will take care of letting you know when you are "an idiot" and when you are on the right track. Don't limit yourself to conversations with perceived "experts." Connect with the wise sage and the clever newbie. Learn from those located next door and those halfway around the planet. Great ideas have no boundaries. *What are people in your ecosystem talking about?*

Show the Way Forward   What transforms leaders into thought leaders is their willingness to bring about something new and then to learn from their early efforts and be willing to share their successes and failures, best practices, and lessons learned so that others don't have to start from scratch when it's their turn.

Thought leaders see their role as more than the leader of one team, one initiative, or one organization. They go further, to show how their experiences can be applied much more broadly. They focus on developing principles, processes, or systems that others can use, expand on, and transform in turn. They identify the right direction, forge into new territory, and then craft the mileposts and chart the way forward for the rest of us. Their goal is for their followers to expand on their efforts and help them create not only incremental change but potentially even a movement. *How can you identify and clarify the short cuts, the best practices, and your lessons learned?*

Here are some other ways to expand your thinking:

- Subscribe to a trend newsletter.[3]
- Attend an industry event or, even better, one far outside your industry. Find opportunities to meet big thinkers from far outside your realm.
- If time or money is an issue, find an online event.
- Convene a thought circle or community of practice with other executives who share your title, job responsibilities, or area of expertise—either inside or outside your organization.
- Find other thought leaders or influencers in your industry and read their latest article or blog post, follow their Twitter stream, or read an article about them.
- Start an online notebook (I like Evernote[4]) to store articles that catch your eye, adding keywords to track topics that interest you.
- Read one book, white paper, or *Harvard Business Review* article every month from someone whom you disagree with, and write a blog post informing others of alternate viewpoints.
- Invite others from your team or organization to a two-hour brainstorming session about the trends—social, technological, political, and economic—that are likely to affect your efforts over the next five years.

- Join a community, nonprofit, or trade association board that is addressing long-term strategic issues in your niche.
- Take a class in a topic that is completely outside your comfort zone, preferably by an instructor who is also an active practitioner in his or her field of expertise.
- Identify a new leader whom you can mentor—and be mentored by.
- Start a meditation practice to give yourself quiet time to rest your mind and make new connections.

Thought Leaders Tell Stories

People of all ages, backgrounds, and traditions respond to great stories. That's the secret behind the enduring power of myths, legends, and scriptures. We see ourselves in stories. We empathize with the heroes and enjoy rooting against the villains. We learn to believe when we observe others' successes, and we overcome doubt when we watch others conquer their obstacles.

Stories are the way we learn.

As you think about your own experiences, those of your team, and those of the people whose lives you have influenced, what stories could you share that will engage and empower and enrich the lives of others? Great storytellers simplify complex information, engage with metaphors, channel universal wisdom, help us understand the potential impact of our efforts, are willing to be vulnerable, and adhere to journalistic principles.

"Uncomplexify"   Avinash Kaushik, author, speaker, and digital marketing evangelist at Google, credits his success (which includes over 200,000 followers on Google+) to his ability to simplify (or as he calls it, "uncomplexify") highly complex information on topics like web analytics and digital marketing into very simple, clear language. He writes his blog, "Occam's Razor,"[5] which has over 100,000 followers, at the fifth-grade level (yes, he even uses a web tool to double-check), yet it attracts Fortune 10 chief marketing officers and beginners alike. He recommends others to follow his lead.[6] Uncomplexifying is not the same as dumbing down—it is simply making the information you are sharing easier for your followers to understand. *How can you simplify your own message?*

Engage with Metaphors   Robin Chase, the cofounder and former CEO of Zipcar, has built a global following for her ideas on sustainability and reducing CO_2 emissions through peer-to-peer networks. She told me, "I constantly pay attention to whether what I'm saying makes sense or not. I'm listening as well as I'm telling. I am a collector of metaphors, always looking for what makes sense for people. I am constantly seeking what resonates with people in terms of the story I'm telling."[7] For example, in a Huffington Post blog post entitled "Fossil Fuel Is the New Slavery: Morally and Economically Corrupt,"[8] Chase uses a metaphor (slavery) that not only captures people's attention but gets them to reexamine their preconceived notions. *What metaphors best explain and engage others with your ideas?*

Channel Universal Wisdom   Chip Conley, the founder and former CEO of Joie de Vivre Hospitality, grew his company into the second-largest boutique hotel group in America. Along the way, he wrote four books about his experiences. He told me, "When I woke up early to write, I often felt that something was coming through me. I believe that being a thought leader is, in some ways, learning how to be a vessel for the great, channeled wisdom that's out there. That somehow it needs to channel through you." He experiences this even more often when he's speaking than when he's writing.[9] *How can you channel the world's wisdom to your audiences?*

Help Others See the Impact   Every year I attend a fundraiser for my favorite local organization, Fresh Lifelines for Youth (FLY), which helps kids stay out of jail by offering them legal education, leadership training, and one-on-one mentoring. At every event, CEO Christa Gannon (who was the recipient of the James Irvine Foundation Leadership Award in 2012) and her team do an excellent job telling stories of the kids who escaped gangs, went back to school, and turned their lives around as a result of participating in FLY's programs. By the end of the breakfast, every attendee pulls out a checkbook—and a big pile of Kleenex. FLY knows that to engage attendees to donate, they need to see a real kid, not a faceless stranger; they need to know that they are having an impact on real lives. If the personal connection is not possible, stories are the next best thing. *Who are the people whose lives you're impacting? How can you engage by telling their stories?*

Be Willing to Be Vulnerable   In 2001, I was invited to speak about women's entrepreneurship at the California Governor's Conference, at the time one of the largest women's conferences in the world. I was on the stage with two business-owners-turned-coauthors and a famous swimsuit-model-turned-successful-entrepreneur. I realized that I had been invited there because I was the "content" speaker—I had lots of great resources to share with women starting their own businesses. But as I listened to the other speakers share their lessons learned, I realized that if I wanted to stand out, I needed to quickly rethink my content-rich presentation style.

So with no planning and no practice, I shared a very personal story. I told the audience about the crossroads I'd faced from age twenty-eight to thirty, when my father became very ill with emphysema, my mother was diagnosed with breast cancer, and my best friend's husband got a brain tumor. During those two years, going from hospital bed to hospital bed, I had had a lot of time to think about whether I was living the life I wanted to be living. I described this as a real turning point that had led me to where I was that day, namely on that stage before them. I then offered my standard entrepreneurial resources, and I closed by saying that while I had lost my dad to his illness, my mother and my best friend's husband were going strong (they still are!), and while I couldn't be thankful, exactly, for what I'd been through, I could certainly appreciate how facing these challenges had led to where I was today.

At the end of that talk, a surprising thing happened. The audience members didn't go talk to the famous swimsuit model; they didn't go to the book signing by the two panelists with the new book: they came and stood in line to talk to me. Dozens and dozens of them. In that moment I realized that it is our personal stories that allow people to connect with us as they recognize themselves in our struggles and journeys. The more we are willing to be vulnerable, the more we connect. *Are you willing to be vulnerable and share your crossroads and lessons learned?*

Practice Journalistic Principles   In his book *Mediactive*, former journalist Dan Gillmor offers a list of principles for thought leaders who contribute to the "emerging ecosystem of knowledge and ideas." These include thoroughness, accuracy, fairness, independence, and transparency.[10] Most of these are self-explanatory, but transparency is more than "tell us who you are, what your interests are and what you believe, so that we can assess the information you've brought us accordingly," as web veteran Jason Fry defines it in his blog post "Transparency Isn't Just for Journalists."[11] I would assert that transparency also requires that we cite or at least credit those whose creativity and innovation have informed our own and delineate what part of our work is original versus what is based on the work of others. Don't hesitate to give credit where credit is due and take credit when you deserve it. *Are you practicing journalistic principles?*

Here are some other ways to learn to tell better stories:

- Attend a storytelling workshop or hire a personal storytelling coach. Doug Stevenson,[12] Lou Heckler,[13] Arina Isaacson,[14] and KC Baker[15] are a few that I recommend.
- Read a book about effective storytelling, like Nancy Duarte's *Resonate*.[16] For other storytelling resources, visit the Thought Leadership Lab website.

- Attend Saul Kaplan's Business Innovation Factory (BIF) storytelling conference in Rhode Island,[17] or a local TED or TEDx event.[18] You can also watch the past BIF and TED events online, which is a great way to observe effective stories well told.
- Watch Brene Brown's TED talk on "The Power of Vulnerability" and think about how vulnerable you are willing to be with the people in your community.[19] (She also has some great books on the same topic, which are well worth reading.)
- Assess your writing with one of the most common readability algorithms, the Flesch Reading Ease, Fog Scale Level, and Flesch-Kincaid Grade Level (you can find them online), to ensure that it stays at about a fifth-grade level.
- Begin to gather your own stories and explore how to tell those stories most effectively. What pictures help you tell the story? Do you need a video or music? Try multiple mechanisms to reach a broader audience.
- In blogs, books, or presentations be sure to cite your sources.

Thought Leaders Build Lasting Relationships

It takes some skill to build a personal relationship from an introduction, and then build an acquaintanceship into an affiliation that is strong enough for the person to be willing to write a check or give his or her time to your cause. Aligning people to your way of thinking or building a movement takes more than getting people to click "Like" on a Facebook page. It takes trust, a long-term view, and an ability to encourage others to spread the word about what you're up to.

Foster Trust   Trust doesn't happen overnight; it is built incrementally, and those who understand the step-by-step nature of relationships are the winners. Guy Kawasaki, the author of *Enchantment: The Art of Changing Hearts, Minds and Actions*, believes that one of the key ways to build trust is to show up—to interact with people.[20] When you share information, listen, and create honest connections, others will perceive your value and that of your ideas; they will get involved and remain engaged over time. To become a trusted thought leader requires not just engaging sporadically with those in your community but being consistently of service and creating sustained connections—remembering that it's not about you, it's about them. *In what ways can you engage and build confidence with others?*

Think Relay, Not Sprint   Creating sustained change or a true movement does not happen overnight either. It takes many allies to bring about change—especially to catalyze sustained transformation in how people think or how things have always been done. Think about the fight for women's right to vote or the efforts to stop the wars in Iraq and Afghanistan. There are many different parts to play: some carry the flame forward, others offer monetary support, still others use their connections, and some serve as critics (yes, we do need critics; they help us to strengthen our arguments). Rather than go it alone, be on the constant lookout for those who may have the interest and skills to take your efforts to the next stage. Be accessible to them. *Who will support your ideas? To whom can you pass the baton?*

Encourage "Others to Others" Conversations   No matter how large your network, you should be building connections to new, potential followers and champions on an ongoing basis. One-to-one conversations are great, but you can't be everywhere. How do you scale your impact by encouraging others to share what you are doing with their networks? It will take a lot of "others to others" conversations to gain momentum for your ideas. Help others understand what's in it for them; create simple messages that are easy to share; and develop engagement strategies that stimulate them to amplify your message. *How can you engage others to spread the word about your ideas?*

Here are other ways to build lasting relationships:

- Set up a mailing list (try iContact, Constant Contact, or AWeber) to help people stay informed on what you're up to.

- Create a place online where people can gather—a LinkedIn group, Facebook fan page, or a simple website based on a free tool like WordPress.com or Wix.com.
- Keep track of who's talking about the topics you care about (use tracking tools like Google Alerts or Newsle). Identify those who are worth meeting or events that are worth attending.
- Make a list of the top three to ten thought leaders in your niche. Subscribe to relevant blogs (try Google blog search) or set up news alerts to let you know when those on your list are speaking in your area or have published a new article or book.
- Find someone who can introduce you to these top thought leaders. LinkedIn is a great tool for identifying those who might connect you.
- If you don't have a personal connection, attend an event in your area where one of these thought leaders is presenting, and introduce yourself.
- Join an industry association, attend or host a Meetup, or attend a conference to make some new connections.
- Create multiple ways that people can engage with your activities—invite them to sign a petition, attend an event, donate, or tell their friends.
- Encourage your followers to share your activities widely—add links to your website, blog, or videos that make it easy for them to forward, comment on, or "Like" something you or others have proposed.

Thought Leaders Share Certain Behaviors

In addition to the specific characteristics we've already been discussing, thought leaders also seem to share a lot of the same behaviors. Rather than stand on a pedestal, they foster approachability. Rather than work in obscurity, they make sure they are "discoverable." Rather than pretending they've got it all figured out, they share their lives openly (the good, the bad, and, within reason, the ugly). Rather than go it alone, they seek support. And rather than staying on the sidelines, they jump in and make things happen. These behaviors have one thing in common: they help thought leaders increase the momentum for their ideas.

Foster Approachability   As a thought leader, you need to know the right people and the right people need to know you. This doesn't mean that you must be an extrovert who collects dozens of business cards at events with no intention of following up. Nor does it mean you only speak to the "most important" people at an event and ignore anyone else when they approach you. Friendliness wins. Whether you're out networking, writing a blog, tweeting up a storm, or hosting a brown-bag lunch, the idea is to attract and connect with followers. That requires you to foster approachability. You will spread your ideas only if others want to speak with you or read what you've written. *Is your writing and speaking style approachable? Are your activities "of service," or are they all about you?*

Be "Discoverable"   Again, thought leadership is as much about whom you know as about who knows you. If your work is invisible to the people who matter, you are not serving yourself or the work you have under way. Your credibility goes up as others know more about you and begin to trust you. As Laura Vanderkam argues in her MoneyWatch article "How to Become a Guru," "If you are quoted in one major news outlet as an expert, chances are you'll soon be quoted in another. . . . [And] once you're quoted in, say, CBS MoneyWatch as a financial guru, it's not just you calling yourself a financial expert. It's a trusted source."[21] Find opportunities to talk to the media. Create a downloadable white paper; document your ideas in a SlideShare or Prezi and share it widely. Apply for an award or ask someone else to nominate you. Google yourself so you can review what others see when they search for you. *What will you do to be more "discoverable" this year?*

Share Openly   Thought leaders cultivate a habit of being pretty transparent about their personal journey. Lynn Price, founder of Camp To Belong, is a great example of someone who willingly shares her own story. Price grew up as a foster child and was separated from her sister when they were both quite young. Her reconnection with her sibling, years later, is at the heart of the work she does today to reconnect separated siblings in foster care. She understands that it is necessary to share her own painful past in order to connect with the campers—letting them know that she's been where they are and helping them to see, through her story, that they might also build a successful life despite their current situation. Her goal is to give them a voice and a reason to be a victor rather than a victim. Her own hero's journey also builds connections with potential donors, volunteers, and policy makers.[22] *How does your personal story impact the work that you do? Will you use your personal experiences to engage people to believe in and align with your ideas?*

Avoid TMI   On the other side of the coin, everyone needs to find his or her own line between what is authentic and will build connections and what is altogether "too much information" (TMI). Penelope Trunk, founder of Brazen Careerist, shares her career advice in over two hundred newspapers.[23] She has no hesitation putting it all out there in the world. Her brand is to tell it like it is—even at the risk of shocking your sensibilities. But Trunk's audience is twenty-somethings. It's hard to shock that crowd. What about your target audience? What constitutes TMI for them? *Before you speak, post, or hit Send, ask yourself, "Would I like to read this on the front page of the* New York Times?"

Be Persistent   I can say with certainty that every thought leader I've ever met has a strong personal drive and a willingness to be persistent. They all want to move the world forward. For some, where that drive came from is easily identifiable. It originated with some life circumstance, obstacle, or setback. For others, they imagine a bigger or a better future than everyone around them. Still others are motivated by a very stubborn belief that "I can do this better." In any case, their determination keeps them focused and unstoppable. *What drives you? Where are you unstoppable?*

Get Support   I can't emphasize enough how important it is to find someone who can support you—a coach, a mentor, or a colleague. You need someone to cheer you on and serve as your sounding board; someone to help you assess your progress. We'll talk about this more throughout the book, but as you set out, take time to develop some milestones and then ask a friend or family member to help you remember to celebrate when you achieve them. Research shows that often by the time we attain our very ambitious goals they seem inevitable. Enlist others to remind you to stop occasionally and appreciate and celebrate your progress before moving forward. *Who can offer you support this year? What milestones will you celebrate?*

Don't Just Think—Do!   Thought leadership is about doing—making change happen in the world. It is not solely about being known as the subject-matter expert or the person who has completed the academic research on what could be done to bring about change. This is not to say you won't think, study, research, and reflect along the way. It also doesn't preclude academics from being thought leaders. But the most effective thought leaders are those who are out in front of their cause, identified as its leader; those willing to show others the way. Firsthand experiences give you the credibility others can rely upon. *Are you in action around your ideas? What are the next steps you can take to build your credibility as someone who is making change happen?*

Now it's time to get started with the first of the seven steps, Find Your Driving Passion. In the next chapter, we'll cover how to identify your niche—your *thought leadership intersection point.* Then we'll explore how to identify and align to trends so that you gain adoption more quickly for your initiatives. And we'll discuss the *What If?* future—the possible future you are committed to bring about.

GETTING STARTED: A QUICK REVIEW

In this chapter we explored:

- An assessment for evaluating your progress to date
- Common characteristics and behaviors of thought leaders
- Resources for expanding your ideas, telling effective stories, and building lasting relationships

CHAPTER 1

FIND YOUR DRIVING PASSION

I am fortunate to have a wonderful mentor, Intrigue Expert and author Sam Horn. She has taught me a lot about the world of thought leadership and urged me to "Find your uniqueness and exploit it in the service of others." We both believe that everyone has a right and a responsibility to be one of a kind. But how do you determine that you *are* one of a kind? How do you find your uniqueness? The first step is to define your niche.

In this chapter we'll cover how to narrow your focus and identify the one or two arenas where you are (or can be) a credible thought leader. Then we'll explore what future you'd like to bring about and what trends you will align to that will ensure your success. We'll also talk about the importance of passion—building your thought leadership in an arena that you care deeply about, one where you are committed to making a difference.

Why is a niche important? Think about the thought leaders we all admire—former president Jimmy Carter, for example. Broadly defined, his post-presidency niche is working for global peace. For

U2's lead singer, Bono, his niche is activism for Africa. Oprah is perhaps best known for her efforts in educating girls. Now I'm not suggesting that any of us will ever be a former president, win twenty-two Grammys, or be a globally recognized television personality (or maybe you will!). But we can take some direction from these examples.

Align your time, energy, and resources around one niche and you'll open far more doors than if you focus in multiple unrelated arenas. You'll have far greater impact and influence and gather much greater attention to your topic, idea, or cause if you don't try to "own" more than one niche. Since few of us have the kind of resources of Carter, Bono, or Oprah, it's all the more imperative that we don't fragment our efforts. Focus your talents in one or only a few arenas; you'll have the chance to make a real difference. (And once you have a well-established platform in one area, it's much easier to broaden to another rather than trying to tackle two at the same time.)

So how do you choose? How do you clarify and crystallize your niche?

Do you already have this figured out? Skip ahead to the section on your *What If?* future. If there is no one obvious arena, topic, or community that you (and others) can call yours, then the next section is for you.

FIND YOUR NICHE

If you have worked in one field for a long time, your niche may already be fairly well established—particularly if you have built a distinguished track record or created a body of work in one arena. But if you've never really thought of your career from the perspective of thought leadership (or if you recently entered or want to enter a new arena), I invite you to use the following exercise to identify your niche.

If you are working with a group of people to develop a thought leadership strategy for your company or your cause, this exercise may serve you better if you broaden the questions and include a wider group rather than just completing it yourself.

Can You Pen Your Venn?

Think back to school when you learned about Venn diagrams. Remember those? Three circles overlying each other with an area in the middle where they all three overlap? In this exercise, the three circles are (1) your expertise or experiences, (2) your credentials, and (3) what you're committed to. The central, overlapping area is what I call your "thought leadership intersection point"—your niche. This intersection point will be an arena that can be uniquely yours, or where you'll be one of the few.

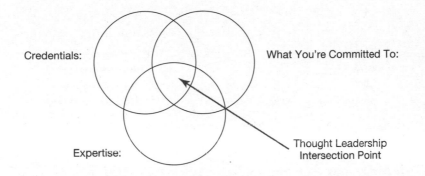

I'll use myself as an example so I can show you what I mean. In 1999, I became one of three or four people in the United States who were established thought leaders in the world of high-growth women's entrepreneurship. (For those who are not familiar with the term *high-growth* in this context, it refers to companies that are funded by equity financing, often angel investment or venture capital, thus allowing the company to grow quickly, often much more quickly than any other type of corporate structure.) I was the CEO of the Forum for Women Entrepreneurs, an organization I had cofounded six years earlier to help women-founded and women-led companies build the knowledge, connections, and gain access to the resources they needed so they could raise equity financing for their companies.

Thus, what I was *committed to* was high-growth women's entrepreneurship—or getting more women entrepreneurs funded. My *credentials*, which helped people believe me to be credible as a thought leader, were that I had an MBA from Stanford; I was the CEO of an organization with a track record of serving women entrepreneurs; and I had cofounded Springboard, the first venture conference for women entrepreneurs. I also had had the *experience* of starting and running a successful business when I was twenty-six; I had worked as a technology executive at several Fortune 500 companies; and I had built a top-notch board for my organization.

My Venn diagram then looked like this:

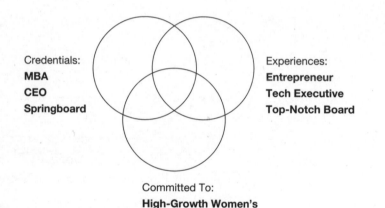

Credentials:
MBA
CEO
Springboard

Experiences:
Entrepreneur
Tech Executive
Top-Notch Board

Committed To:
High-Growth Women's
Entrepreneurship

I can't pretend that I understood all this back then. It was the outside world that defined my niche for me—particularly the press when they called me as a subject-matter expert on the dot-com boom and women entrepreneurs. I was then able to build on that credibility as I began to develop my own point of view about how the future should unfold and what changes were needed so that more women entrepreneurs could get funded. But that's jumping ahead; let's focus on *you* now.

How to Pen Your Venn

Ready to create your own Venn diagram? Get out a copy of your resume or bio, a highlighter, and some paper and begin to answer the following questions. Create as complete a list as you can and don't hesitate to use multiple pages.

Step 1: What Are Your Credentials?   Depending on your career choices, you may have gained your credentials by the letters after your name, by what jobs you've held, what licenses or certificates you've completed, or what status you've achieved in your organization. That said, I use the term *credentials* broadly—it doesn't imply only people with a formal education. I have met amazing thought leaders without a high school diploma. Here are a few things to think about as you complete this exercise.

As an executive, your credentials are often denoted by job title or rank, by the teams you've led or been a part of, the deals you've closed, the products you've shipped, or the services you've developed. If you've worked at Fortune 500 companies, that can add a certain amount of credibility as well.

As an entrepreneur, your credentials are most often tied to the revenue, brand, or popularity of your company or products. They can also be tied to the amount of money you raised or a successful exit you helped achieve. Serial entrepreneurs, even when they have had one spectacular failure, have stronger credentials than first-time CEOs.

As a community or nonprofit leader, your credentials include your title or rank, the size and reputation of your organization, and the type of challenge that you are tackling, as well as the impact you and your organization have had in that arena.

As a service provider, in addition to any professional certifications you've received, your credentials are defined by your title and rank but also by the size and reputation of your organization and that of your clients.

As an academic, in addition to your degrees, the reputation of your institution and your own rank within that institution are often your strongest credentials.

No matter which career choice you've made, other ways you may have established your credentials are by materials you've written (articles, white papers, books, blogs, research papers), awards or honors you've received, or other associations that you've affiliated with or where you have taken a leadership role.

Think objectively and imagine what others who know you well might say about you. Jot down everything that comes to mind. Don't limit yourself to work arenas. Add any leadership roles you've held, even as a volunteer.

Step 2: What Is Your Expertise or Unique Experience?

Next start a new page and write down your areas of expertise and your unique experiences. Again we are not thinking narrowly here. What skills do you have; what events have you lived through; what talents have you developed? Have you had a unique experience—a transformative experience—that set you on a new path? What is one topic around which you are the guru? Have you invented anything or been the first to accomplish something? Are you more knowledgeable than 95 percent of the world about something? Have you survived or overcome something and then learned some lessons?

Where have you lived or traveled? Anywhere unusual? Have you completed significant research in an arena or figured out how to do something that others don't know how to do? Have you started a company or organization, led a merger, built a product, managed an initiative? Are you a great public speaker or storyteller, a renowned expert in cheese, or in command of more hockey statistics than anyone who ever lived? Write it down! What do others call you about to get your advice or counsel? What are you the known (or budding) expert in? What makes you stand out from the crowd? If you want more questions to spark your thinking, see "More Food for Thought" at the end of the chapter.

Step 3: What Are You Committed to or Passionate About?   Before we jump into this next part of the exercise, I want to set the stage by sharing a quote with you from the first female chief of the Cherokee Nation, Wilma Mankiller: "The happiest people I've ever met, regardless of their profession, their social standing, or their economic status, are people that are fully engaged in the world around them. The most fulfilled people are the ones who get up every morning and stand for something larger than themselves. They are the people who care about others, who will extend a helping hand to someone in need or will speak up about an injustice when they see it."[1] I couldn't have said it better myself.

What do *you* stand for? Take a new piece of paper and write down the things that you're passionate about and committed to. Where do you devote your time, even when no one is willing to pay you? What group of people do you stand for and with? What can you speak about at length if someone gives you an opening? What is the one problem that you want to help solve, one situation that is occurring that you'd like to see halted, or one arena where new possibilities are opening up that you'd like to be the first to understand? Where do you disagree with the accepted point of view? Where do you see a new way of doing things that others don't yet see? How would you like to transform people's way of thinking?

What would others say you're committed to that you haven't included? In the last three months, what have you spent your spare time doing? What topics do you find yourself drawn to when you're standing in the library, selecting a TV show, or reading a magazine? What problems are happening in your industry or in your state that you'd like to have an impact on? Think about challenges or problems you've helped to solve (or want to solve) in your company, region, or school district. What about bigger challenges you've been involved with—political, economic, environmental?

Think broadly; there are no limits here. Make a long list, maybe thirty or forty items. Whatever gets you up in the morning, whatever lights you up and makes you willing to fight for a cause or an issue you believe in, could go on the list. If you want more questions to spark your thinking, see "More Food for Thought" at the end of the chapter.

Step 4: Narrow and Hone   Now you are going to hone and narrow to find three potential arenas where you could develop your thought leadership. Start with your last list (what you're committed to) first. You're going to go through the list four times.

- The first time, cross off the things that at one time you cared a lot about or were committed to but that are no longer in your sweet spot or something you want to focus on.
- The second time through, put a star next to each item that is really important to you. (If you have only a few items left, skip the next step.)
- The third time through the list, take a highlighter and highlight up to ten items from the starred choices that are areas where you might be willing to develop yourself as a thought leader over the next one to three years.
- Finally, select the top three items on the list that you are most committed to and prioritize them 1, 2, and 3.

Step 5: Identify the "Reasons to Believe"   Now that you have identified three potential areas that you are committed to, the next step is to determine the reasons others should listen to you on these topics. This is what advertisers call the "reasons to believe." What experiences, expertise, know-how, and credentials make you believable as the best person (or one of the best) to speak out about these topics?

Before we get to the specifics, I want to add one caveat. Since you may be at the beginning of your thought leadership journey, I don't want you to give up if you don't have a whole list of credentials and expertise yet to support the niche that you most care about. You will need to build some of those "reasons to believe" over time (or align with a partner that has more credibility). We all start somewhere. Rather than think about giving up, think of creating a road map to help you plan the steps you need to take for others to believe you, rely on you, and identify you as the guru within your niche.

Let's return to your top three items:

- Take a new piece of paper and write the number one item you're committed to at the top. Review your list of credentials and identify those that most give you credibility when you are speaking about this item. Copy these credentials to the page. Next review your list of expertise and experiences and copy those that best align to or inform your point of view.
- Take a second piece of paper and write down the second-most important item you are committed to. Review your list of credentials and experiences. Copy the most relevant items to this sheet as you did above. (Note: There may be overlap from the previous list.)
- Take a third piece of paper and write down the third-most important item you are committed to. Repeat the steps above.

Step 6: Is There an Audience or Market Need?   Now that you have narrowed your lists, determined where you have the strongest commitment, and identified your related credentials and expertise, the last step in identifying your niche is to determine if there is an audience (or market need) in that area.

It is easy to overlook this step. Developing your reputation as a thought leader does not happen overnight—it takes time, attention, and focus. You can choose from a lot of arenas. To maximize your outcomes, choose one arena that meets some or all of the following criteria:

- There is a large and preferably growing interest in this arena— in your company, industry, or region. (What you define as "large" may vary, but if only five people care, it doesn't matter much if you're the go-to person on that topic.)

- You are (or could be) one of the first or few to be known in this niche.
- There is a real problem in this arena that you want to solve or a challenge that you have the unique skills to address.
- You have a distinct point of view that is unique or counter to the expected wisdom.

At the completion of this exercise, you should have identified at least one topic or arena where you want to be the go-to person and which has a significant and growing group of people who share your interest. Hopefully, you have also identified some "reasons to believe" that will back up your expertise in that arena. Test your final selections with a few close associates. Would they have chosen that arena for you? Can they add anything to the reasons to believe in you?

If you are a little stuck, ask one of your colleagues or associates if he or she would be willing to get together for an hour so that you can both develop your thought leadership niche. Walk through the exercise together and discuss each section—first for one of you and then the other. Ask your buddy for their thoughts and suggestions along the way. Invite them to push you to think big!

If you're finding it challenging to complete the Venn exercise because you absolutely hate to narrow your options and opportunities in any way, I understand. I tend towards that direction myself—I like to play outside the lines (or the circles). But that can also be limiting. If others don't know what your niche is, they are less likely to send you the people you really need to meet—people who could hire you, present you with new opportunities, buy what you're selling, or help you achieve the future you envision.

The goal of the Pen Your Venn exercise is to define a niche you can play in, not because it will limit you but because it will broaden your opportunities to be the trusted source and the go-to expert. Having a clearly defined niche will expand the likelihood that you'll be able to have a meaningful impact in the world.

Now let's talk about what that impact might look like. What would you like the future to be?

ENVISION YOUR *WHAT IF?* FUTURE

One of the Silicon Valley giants, venture capitalist Vinod Khosla, believes, "Great leaders invent the future they want."[1] He should know! He is a cofounder of Sun Microsystems, one of the early technology success stories, and has since funded numerous other entrepreneurial ventures, helping simple ideas turn into highly successful companies that continue to shape the future.

But what if anyone could invent a possible future and be a part of making it a reality? This is what I call envisioning your *What If?* future (WIF). A WIF is a single, simple, striking description or image of the future you want to see. All thought leaders need a WIF. They may not yet be sure how to get there, but an inspiring WIF can attract followers and galvanize them to take action.

In 1993, a simple statistic galvanized me into action. Less than 1 percent of the venture capital funding in the United States was going to women entrepreneurs. When my friends and I started the Forum for Women Entrepreneurs (FWE), the *What If?* future we envisioned was "What if women received 50 percent of the venture capital funding in the United States?" I called it "changing the poster" because if you had lined up all the folks who received venture funding for their businesses in 1993, the picture would have been 99 percent men. I wanted a lot more women on that poster.

The cofounders of FWE had impressive credentials: most of us had MBAs from top schools and years of corporate and entrepreneurial experience. We had deep expertise in the issues of building high-growth ventures, and we were all very committed to the success of women as entrepreneurs. But it was our WIF that really helped us to bring others on board.

Even if you don't have a lot of credentials and expertise but you have identified a clear *What If?* future, it is more than possible to become the go-to person in a niche—particularly if it's a pretty exciting future you are working to create. Others will get on board simply because they want to be a part of bringing it about. Over time, you'll attain credentials and expertise by the actions you take to bring about that future.

Here are other examples of inspiring, even world-changing WIFs:

1. *Maria Montessori* (the creator of Montessori education): What would it look like if we created a classroom where children are rewarded for independence of thinking and acting?
2. *Robin Chase* (founder and former CEO of Zipcar, the world's largest car-sharing service, and now CEO of Buzzcar, a peer-to-peer car rental company): What would the world look like if we replaced the industrial economy with a collaborative economy?
3. *Chip Conley* (founder and former CEO of Joie de Vivre Hospitality): What if we could structure a company so that every employee feels as if they are living their calling, from the hotel manager to the housekeeper?

Some people call their idealized future their "vision," but I find that *"What If? future"* more quickly encapsulates what I'm talking about. Many people get hung up on the word "vision." It can feel too nebulous, too pie-in-the-sky, or even a bit foolish to say, at the beginning of a thought leadership journey, "This is my vision." Even those who understand the importance of having a vision may not be ready to state one publicly.

Starting with a clear WIF question has several advantages. Your *What If?* question—especially if it's a big, seemingly unanswerable one—can open the door to conversations. Those conversations in turn will help you identify who might align with you and who won't. Over time, you will begin to crystallize your thinking into what can more clearly be called a Vision, with a capital V, which will include a plan for how you want to bring it about.

Define Your *What If?* Future

So how do you define your WIF? Start with the third circle in your Venn diagram—what you are committed to. With that in mind, answer these questions:

- What future am I committed to making happen in this arena?
- What if I could make one change related to this issue or problem? What would that be?
- What future do I stand for? What will I work to eradicate?
- What must happen? What do I want to make happen?
- What must I work to prevent from happening? What must no longer be allowed to happen?
- What injustices am I committed to correct within this arena?
- What malfeasance am I committed to undo within my community, company, or industry?
- What "way it's always been done" is no longer the way it should be done?
- What do people not know yet that they must be informed about?
- What amazing transformation has already occurred that I know about and that needs to be shared more broadly?
- What new way of doing things have I created (or learned about) that needs to be more broadly adopted?
- What future do I envision that others don't yet see?
- What legacy do I want to leave?

Have some fun with this exercise—push yourself to think big and then bigger. Don't think exclusively about the next few months; think about the next few years or even decades. What improvement do you want to see in the world? What advancements are you already a part of bringing about? What progress do you already have under way in your organization or volunteer activities? What scares you a bit to take on? What inspires and energizes you to get moving? What are the boundaries of what is possible today and how can you push those boundaries?

If you find yourself constrained by all the potential challenges to accomplishing this WIF, start a separate page and jot all of these thoughts down in one place. Give yourself permission to consider them later rather than be overwhelmed today by all the reasons a better future is not possible. Stay focused on creating a WIF that is exciting and energizing, one that you would like to devote some time and energy to bring about.

This is not a onetime exercise—you won't necessarily be able to clarify a long-term future the first time you complete the exercise. Talk to more people. Do more research. Come back to these questions, iteratively, until a WIF emerges that seizes your imagination.

And don't worry if you don't yet "know." You'll figure it out! As you listen to and learn from others and from your own experiences, you will be able to revise and deepen and broaden your thinking. You simply have to give yourself permission to explore the known and test today's limits and boundaries.

Think Big

Although you may not recognize the parallel at first, there is a lot of similarity (and overlap) between thought leaders and early-stage entrepreneurs. In both cases, the key to success is to think *big*.

Over the last twenty years, I have sat through many hundreds of hours of entrepreneurs pitching their business ideas to potential investors, and one thing I've learned: the bigger the idea, and sometimes the more crazy and improbable it might be, the more likely you are to get funding.

Now to many of us that seems counterintuitive. Why would someone want to invest in something big that has very little certainty of coming to pass when they could invest in a more incremental, milestone improvement that is absolutely possible?

I would give two answers to that. The first one may seem to have less relevance to your situation if you are not seeking venture funding, but hang in with me for a minute. Venture capital funders always want the possibility of a big return on their investments—10x to

100x returns—in order to make up for the many investments they make that have no return at all. If they invest in an incremental idea, there is very little possibility they will have an outsize win. This is true for all of us: if we don't invest our time, energy, and resources in big futures—even crazy futures—there is little chance that they will come about by accident.

Second, investors want to be inspired. Big ideas inspire.

People with big ideas inspire not just investors; they inspire us all—even if we think they're grandiose, over the top, or unachievable. We want to engage to make a big *What If?* future possible. After all, it often takes almost as much work to achieve something small as it does to have a big impact. When we can envision a big possible win sometime in the future, we are more likely to join others to make it happen. One group that has been amazingly successful at envisioning a big *What If?* future and galvanizing thousands to help bring it about are the leaders of the global environmental sustainability organization, the Pachamama Alliance.

The Pachamama Alliance was originally founded in the 1990s by a group of people from the United States, including Bill and Lynne Twist and John Perkins, and the elders of the Achuar, an indigenous people in the Amazon rainforest of Ecuador and Peru. Over the next twenty years, their combined efforts protected over 3 million acres of Amazon rainforest from oil development. The Alliance is committed to environmental sustainability through activism, education, and advocacy. But the founding idea that the Achuar elders posed to their U.S. colleagues was a much bigger WIF question: How do we transform the culture of overconsumption around the globe in order to save the rainforest?

This big WIF idea has attracted millions of dollars in private contributions, thousands of global partners, and hundreds of thousands of volunteer hours. Pachamama volunteers and staff have hosted symposia, workshops, and training programs in more than seven countries. In 2012 alone, they trained over 3,500 volunteer facilitators worldwide. They also took hundreds of people to visit the rainforest to engage them firsthand in the Achuar culture.

With a cause this big, the Pachamama team knows there's no time to think small. They also know that many share their dream of a world without overconsumption. Their WIF may feel impossible, but it is worthy of the time, energy, money, and devotion it will take to achieve.

Now lest I scare you off with this story, let me assure you that your WIF does not have to be anywhere near this big. Not everyone is ready to tackle global overconsumption and save the planet. There are many engaging and energizing *What If?* futures that start (and end) much closer to home. Think about what poster you'd like to change or what you'd like to improve in your community, company, or industry.

Creating your WIF is an iterative process. Keep pushing yourself, and your team if you have one, to imagine an ever bigger future.

No idea yet what your WIF is? Get out and talk to people. Read blogs, books, or commentary that align with—or argue against—your thinking on a subject. Stop by the Pachamama site to get inspired (http://www.pachamama.org), or watch some TED talks (http://www.ted.com/talks). There you will find many visionary thinkers with big ideas. You'll not only be inspired; you'll also begin to observe some of the trends forming in the world that you may want to align with, or work against.

ALIGN WITH (OR BUCK) TRENDS

Aligning yourself with emerging trends can inspire and inform your WIF. It can also help you overcome the natural resistance to change, whether in your audience, in the larger world, or in your own thinking. Think of what happens when you ride close behind another bicyclist: you don't have to work as hard, because the bicyclist in front of you serves as a windbreak, reducing your air resistance. Experienced bicyclists take advantage of this effect—they call it "drafting off" each other.[2] How can you draft off the momentum of others?

By aligning with the global trend towards sustainability, the Pachamama Alliance is able to attract a very large following to their efforts. My own efforts in support of women entrepreneurs were pushed forward by the dot-com frenzy in Silicon Valley in 1999.

What trends will you align with?

Identify Key Trends

Most of the time the trends are pretty obvious (that's why they're called trends). They're wherever the conversation is happening now. You can think of the following as a market research exercise. Make notes on the trends you're uncovering in a spreadsheet or use Evernote. As you continue to notice and understand trends that are emerging or evolving, add to your notes.

- Look for Facebook, Google+, or LinkedIn groups or meetups related to your Venn circles. What do people talk about in these gatherings?
- Go to Google or Twitter and type in some of the words, phrases, or keywords from your circles. Try the words separately and together. Try different combinations. Note the main topics and trends that are being discussed. What other keywords are related?
- Peruse a trade magazine, conference brochure, or website to learn what topics are being discussed.
- Seek out continuing education or webinar topics from your industry association.
- Identify a top expert in your arena and study what she or he is talking about.
- If you know someone who teaches in your niche, ask what new topics are being discussed in the classroom. If you teach in your niche, explore this question with your colleagues.
- Subscribe to a futurist newsletter.[3]
- Browse the funding pitches on Indiegogo or Kickstarter.[4]

Answer the following questions:

- What economic trends might have an impact (positive or negative) on whether my WIF will be possible?
- What local, regional, national, and global political trends might impact my WIF?
- What are the technological trends, and at what speed will new technologies begin to have an impact? What technology advancements will be needed to ensure that my WIF will be possible?
- What client, customer, vendor, market, and industry trends will impact my WIF?
- What local, regional, national, and global social trends may impact my WIF?
- What regulatory or legislative changes are under way?
- What trending meme, fad, style, perspective, or point of view is getting the most attention?

If you know the current trends in your arena, and their boundaries, you can push others to think in new ways, often far beyond what appear to be today's limitations. That's why determining the trends in your own industry is so valuable. Please don't skip this exercise. Stop and think through what trends you can align with that will move your efforts forward more quickly.

I realize that you may be thinking, "I don't want to be a lemming. I don't want to go along with the trends. In fact, I'm known as someone who bucks the trends and goes my own way." Great! There's nothing wrong with that.

Being counterintuitive or the dissident voice will definitely help you stand out and get noticed. People won't necessarily agree with you, and that's fine too. Those who buck the trends often make the most progress—they help people question the status quo and view things in a new light.

After all, we thought leaders are change-makers. We want to see (and make) the world go in a new direction.

While the world's leaders are calling for more oil development, the Pachamama Alliance advocates a different direction: curbing our overconsumption so that we don't need more oil. Its efforts have put it up against significant opponents, including major oil companies and the governments that support them. But the Alliance continues the fight—it's epic, it's daring, and it's worth it.

Another countertrend winner is Southwest Airlines. Going against his industry's trend for higher and higher baggage fees, Southwest's CEO Gary Kelly made the decision not to charge passengers to check their luggage. Why? Because he didn't want to turn Southwest flight attendants into baggage handlers, as passengers tried to stuff more and more luggage into the overhead bins. "That would make the flight attendants unhappy," said Kelly. "And that in turn would make passengers unhappy. We want our employees to feel that their job is a calling, and the people who most have to feel that way are the ones closest to the customer."[5] Now there's a rare, counterintuitive attitude: employees and customers over bottom line profits. Let's hope he eventually gets the whole airline industry on his side.

Lynn Price, the founder of Camp To Belong, has also worked against the trends since 1995, when she started the first summer camp for foster kids who had been separated from their siblings. Legislation and prevailing wisdom of the time said it was better that kids had foster homes rather than worry much about whether they ever saw their siblings again. Yet, Lynn's personal experience of being separated from her own sister as a child told her this practice was outdated and ultimately caused great harm to foster siblings.

Lynn's long-term *What If?* future remains the passage of legislation that will reverse the cruel practice of separating siblings when they are placed in foster care. In the meantime, she has spent years building a place for foster siblings to come together for summer fun. Today, Camp To Belong hosts ten programs across the United States and Australia. Price knows that her *What If?*

future will take years to achieve, and she believes that every Camp To Belong experience builds more momentum for her cause (http://www.camptobelong.org). *How can you buck conventional wisdom or push against prevailing trends?*

Now that you have identified your niche, crystallized your *What If?* future, and determined which trends you will align with or against, you are ready to move on to the next chapter. There we'll explore how you can begin to bring about that future, how to create and test possible transformative ideas and bring about the first ripples of change in your company, industry, or community.

FIND YOUR DRIVING PASSION: A QUICK REVIEW

In this step of the thought leadership journey, successful thought leaders

- Identify the "thought leadership intersection point," where their credentials, expertise, and commitments are aligned
- Envision the *What If?* future that they stand for and are ready to make happen
- Think big, creating a *What If?* future that inspires and engages others
- Identify the economic, political, technological, and other trends that they can align with or that they will work against

MORE FOOD FOR THOUGHT

Pen Your Venn

If you would like additional questions to jog your memory or open up your imagination when you're doing the Pen Your Venn exercise, you'll find more below.

Credentials Questions

- What are some of your recent job titles?
- What industries have you worked in?
- Have you ever been named to a top 10 or 100 list? For what?
- Do you have an advanced degree? What in?
- Have you received any certifications?
- Have you filed for any patents? In what area(s)?
- Have you ever started a company or run a division? What was it?
- Have you served on a board or advisory board?

Expertise Questions

- When people say you're always in the know about something, what is that?
- What subjects have you written about for publication?
- If you were asked to write an article about something, what would it be?
- If you asked ten people to complete this sentence, "She/he is the best person I know at ..." what would they say?
- What are you most proud to have achieved?
- Have you been invited to speak or write about any topics recently?
- What are your core professional skills sets? Personal attributes?

(continued)

- What do you know that others don't really know much about?
- Where are you considered a leader?
- Have you developed a new way of doing things? In what arena?

Commitment Questions

- What do you read about when you have a few spare moments?
- What do you think needs to be fixed or improved in the world?
- Complete these sentences:
  - Nothing makes me happier than working on ...
  - What I really care about is ...
  - Nothing gets me out of bed faster than my commitment to ...
  - What gives me goose bumps is imagining ...
  - I have unique ideas about ...

CHAPTER 2

BUILD YOUR RIPPLES OF INFLUENCE

Creating a movement requires that you build a series of ever expanding circles of change—adjustments in how people think, act, and see the world. Think of it as drops of water falling one by one into a large pool. The first drop causes a disturbance on the surface that ripples out. Then another drop begins a second circle inside the first one. As that expands, a third takes its place.

As each circle grows and expands, other drops create more and more ripples until the entire pool is a swirl. All the drops, taken together, have an impact far beyond what could initially be extrapolated from the size of any one small drop on its own.

Each of us individually is only one small drop of water, and our impact may be pretty small. In fact, when you're in the middle of creating a revision or improvement to the status quo, you may not realize you are having an impact at all. You may be so head-down, focused, and engaged with the efforts you have under way that you don't even know that you've already begun to make a difference.

It's hard to recognize that you might have launched a ripple that could, over time, become a widely adopted initiative, a new way of thinking, or even a full-blown movement.

In the last chapter, you identified your "thought leadership intersection point." Think of that as the selection of your pond. And the *What If?* future you defined? That's the shore where you'd like your ripples (your impact) to lead. But when you have a big *What If?* future (WIF), reaching the far shore will not happen overnight. Instead you'll need to determine where you are going to start—what first efforts should you undertake to move your WIF from a possibility into a reality? Then you'll need to identify who can join your efforts so that together you can cause a big enough wave to make a real difference.

In this chapter, we'll explore how you can identify, test, and refine your initial ideas, learning from and listening to those who can inform your decision process. Initially, your momentum may be slow; it may develop in fits and starts. So we'll also talk about how to systematically build enough momentum around one small idea that it becomes a big idea worth moving forward.

Each of the steps you'll learn in this and the next few chapters is iterative. Taking and retaking these steps, you will create the first and subsequent ever-expanding circles in your pond. As you bring more and more supporters on board with your ideas and enlist them to add their efforts to yours, you will create your first ripples of change. When you teach and empower others to recreate what you've initiated, their ripples will build on and reinforce your own, creating a surge of momentum.

If you are just beginning your thought leadership journey, read the next section with a view to how to identify and test new ideas that address the challenges and opportunities you have identified. If you have already established your track record in one company, community, or organization, you will use the same process to test and clarify what you've learned and accomplished there so that you can begin to "take it on the road" to have a broader impact in your industry or niche. Either way, then, you'll need to go through the same exercises to scale your impact to the next level and bring about your WIF.

START YOUR FIRST RIPPLES

Where will you start? What should you do today to generate your first ripples in the pond? I urge you to begin by sharing your *What If?* future with as many people as possible—by expanding your "adjacent possible," assembling a bricolage of ideas, and nurturing consilient and divergent thinking.

Expand Your "Adjacent Possible"

The reality is, there are dozens, hundreds, even thousands of paths that might lead to the *What If?* future you have identified. Let me use the example of FWE, the organization I led for ten years, to explain. As I mentioned before, the basis for founding FWE was the core statistic that in 1993 less than 1 percent of the venture capital funding in the United States was going to women entrepreneurs. My cofounder, Jennifer Gill Roberts, learned that statistic when she was in her second year at Stanford Business School. As the daughter of a venture capitalist, Roberts found that information both unexpected and downright alarming. She knew she wanted to do something about it. But what? Where should she even begin?

As an MBA student, Roberts had the opportunity to do an independent study on the topic for one quarter. She invited about fifteen women she knew to become her advisors as she explored what could be done. The initial advisory team included CEOs, venture capitalists, attorneys, bankers, and accountants. These were all people who cared about and were motivated to address this imbalance in the market.

Over the next few months, the team came together and explored a number of possibilities. Should Roberts start a woman-focused venture fund so they could directly provide funding to women entrepreneurs? Should she start an angel group or an advocacy organization?

At the same time, Roberts was looking into why women entrepreneurs were not getting any money. What she discovered was that there were three key ingredients missing from the equation. Women lacked the know-how on venture capital; they lacked access to the resource providers—attorneys, accountants, and bankers, for example—that helped venture-funded businesses be successful; and they lacked connections to other women entrepreneurs who had successfully raised venture financing.

As the quarter came to an end, Roberts had learned a great deal and she was very motivated to act, but she was not convinced a venture fund, angel group, or advocacy organization was the way to go. She moved on to other projects, including landing a job as a venture capitalist in a well-known firm (although not one focused on funding women). But she kept getting calls from the advisors she had convened. They wanted to know what she was doing to move forward—how could they help?

Over the summer after completing business school, Roberts asked me to sit down with her to explore some options she was still considering. What if she were to start an organization that addressed the three systemic issues underlying women's insignificant share of the venture funding pie? What if the organization helped women learn more about how to raise money, and gave them access to the right resources, and then connected them with one another? Was I interested in being involved? I was immediately enrolled, and that was the beginning of the Forum for Women Entrepreneurs (originally the Silicon Valley Women Entrepreneurs).

The entire process took about nine months from the time Roberts first began her independent study project until we hosted our first event in October 1993. The process was iterative: she had probably a hundred different conversations (or more) about the WIF she envisioned. She got input from men and women, experienced sages and start-up newbies, investors and service providers and longtime CEOs. She kept pushing until she found a way forward to that WIF—a future she believed in and one she felt had a chance to make a real difference. And it did. Over the next few years, the Forum for Women Entrepreneurs helped women raise many millions for their businesses, and we had a meaningful impact on that 1 percent statistic.

Most Thought Leadership Lab clients are in a situation similar to Jennifer Gill Roberts's. They see an injustice, challenge, or even a big opportunity that is right in front of them, but they are completely unsure of what to do about it. They often have the skills and credentials to bring about the *What If?* future they envision, but they are not sure where to start.

How do you narrow down to one transformative kernel of an idea that will be the effort you lead to bring about your WIF? Here we need to take some lessons from the world of innovation. In his book *Where Good Ideas Come From*, popular science writer Steven Johnson describes what he calls the "adjacent possible"—a possible shadow future that is just beyond our reach. Johnson contends that there are many different ways the world may unfold or reinvent itself, but the space of reinvention is not infinite—only certain things can happen.

He says, "Think of [the future] as a house that magically expands with each door you open. You begin in a room with four doors, each leading to a new room that you haven't visited yet. Those four rooms are the *adjacent possible*. But once you open one of those doors and stroll into that room, three new doors appear, each leading to a brand-new room that you couldn't have reached from your original starting point. Keep opening new doors and eventually you'll have built a palace."[1]

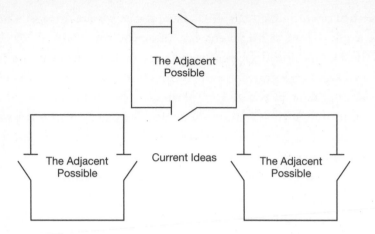

I love the idea that each of us is building our own WIF palace—opening more and more doors to explore an ever-expanding adjacent possible. For Roberts, those doors opened when she created an advisory council: each of the council members gave her new ideas, introduced her to other people, and helped her explore each option in turn. Her job was simply to share with them her *What If?* future—"What if we could significantly increase the amount of venture funding received by women entrepreneurs?"—and let the possibilities unfold.

How can you expand your own adjacent possible? You must share your WIF with many different people. I realize this can take real courage, since we risk having our half-baked ideas ridiculed and criticized. But we also open ourselves to the possibility that our ideas might come to fruition—with help from others. After all, solutions don't usually emerge in isolation. *What will you do today to expand your adjacent possible?*

Assemble Your Bricolage

"We have a natural tendency to romanticize breakthrough innovations," Steven Johnson continues in an interview about his book, "imagining momentous ideas transcending their surroundings . . . . But ideas are works of *bricolage* (French, for 'something constructed from whatever items are on hand'). They are, almost inevitably, networks of other ideas. We take the ideas we've inherited or stumbled across, and we jigger them together into some new shape."[2]

Think of Rube Goldberg. By combining lots of everyday objects, he created magical (and seemingly impossible) functioning machines. Similarly, thought leaders assemble their own magical new concepts, programs, projects, and products when they are willing to share their initial kernel of an idea with others and then build in and build on their input and opinions to create a new, unique, and innovative bricolage. That was certainly the case for my client Van Ton-Quinlivan.

CASE STUDY: VAN TON-QUINLIVAN

When Van Ton-Quinlivan came to the United States from Vietnam at the age of six, no one could have predicted she would be appointed by Governor Jerry Brown to be the vice chancellor for California's community colleges, the largest community college system in the world, by the time she was forty-three. Looking back, she knows that it was bringing together the ideas and interests of many different people into her successful PowerPathway program, and then scaling that program across her industry, that led to her becoming a recognized thought leader in her niche and placed her in line for the vice chancellor appointment.

Ton-Quinlivan and her family escaped to the United States during the Vietnam War. She spoke no English, and although her family arrived in the country intact, they had lost everything. Despite these setbacks, Ton-Quinlivan went on to graduate as the valedictorian of her high school class, attend Georgetown University, and receive two master's degrees from Stanford—an MBA and a Masters of Education.

Informed by her experiences, Ton-Quinlivan knew the important role education played in giving people access to economic opportunity and a new chance; this was particularly true for diverse students from disadvantaged backgrounds. At Stanford, she studied educational reform, and later she taught part-time in a community college.

In 2007, after a variety of corporate roles, Ton-Quinlivan was recruited to join Pacific Gas and Electric (PG&E), one of the country's largest utilities. One year later, she called me for some career advice. We agreed that one of her options—helping disadvantaged workers secure positions at PG&E—gave her a clear opportunity to make an enduring impact in workforce development, an arena that really mattered to her.

From the first, it was clear to me that Ton-Quinlivan had the passion and commitment to make a real difference in this role, given her personal history. She also had the credentials and experience to be credible in her arena. In addition, the company was facing a looming problem that gave her lots of leeway to act. As she explained, "The baby boomers were beginning to age out. All across the energy sector, between 25 percent and 50 percent of the workforce was on the verge of becoming retirement eligible. Within the next five to ten years these workers would be exiting the workplace, taking their extensive experience with them, and we would need to replenish them with new skilled workers."

Ton-Quinlivan came to her new role with a unique WIF: could she find a way to not only recruit new skilled workers to PG&E but also create new pathways for diverse and disadvantaged candidates? "For years the company had struggled to find diverse candidates for entry-level positions," she explained. Many different programs had been tried, but none had been successful so far.

She had a new approach. "I had seen a model of collaboration in the biotech industry that would actually yield us the diverse, qualified candidate pool we needed." She knew that by bringing together industry, community colleges, and the workforce investment system (a statewide network of organizations that help displaced workers train for and find jobs), PG&E could prepare displaced workers, including veterans, for jobs in the utility industry, exactly as the biotech industry had done. She proposed that the company launch a new workforce development program called PowerPathway (see the diagram in Chapter Five).

But having a great idea, even a proven approach, was not enough. After all, PG&E was a one-hundred-year-old company, highly regulated and slow to adopt new ideas. "That's not how things are done around here," was the constant refrain she heard in her initial forays to bring others on board with her efforts.

She persevered. "I started with no resources at all. All I had was an understanding that the company was facing an enormous challenge and I knew that no one was looking at it the same way I was," Ton-Quinlivan explained. "I set up meetings one by one with people I knew within the company whose roles in some way were impacted by the upcoming tidal wave of retirements." Through these meetings Ton-Quinlivan gained a clearer picture of who was interested in aligning with her to make PowerPathway a success, and who was open to try something new that had never been done before. They became her internal stakeholders.

Next she enlisted regional stakeholders, including community college presidents, leaders of veterans' organizations, and directors of local workforce investment boards. "Each of these supporters joined my efforts for different reasons—some because they wanted to help veterans find jobs, some because they wanted to be affiliated with the efforts of a large local employer. Others joined us because of my personal connection with them or my company's reputation. And some came on board because they had funding for community workforce initiatives."

None of them had ever seen a program like PowerPathway before. But Ton-Quinlivan shared with them the success of the program in the biotech industry, and she used her personal credibility to raise awareness and engage initial interested parties.

In order to build momentum within her own company, she went further, identifying and meeting separately with five senior vice presidents to determine what their individual needs were. She then incorporated their interests into her plan.

"I learned you have to enlist all these stakeholders in the design of your program, not in a way that would water it down, but so that it serves the interest of many parties. This is especially true when you're trying to do something intrapreneurial." By integrating all of the senior VPs' interests into the design of PowerPathway, the program would now meet the goals and align the interests of five different departments in the company as well as a broad set of regional constituencies. This allowed her to overcome many of the internal and external naysayers.

The wide buy-in for the program not only assured its success; it also gave Ton-Quinlivan a number of avenues for championing PG&E's efforts more widely. The senior VPs, local community colleges, workforce organizations, and local veterans groups were eager to trumpet the launch of PowerPathway programs across California. When the program had successes—including job placements for recently returned veterans into high-paying jobs—these constituents helped her spread the word.

Media opportunities soon came her way along with speaking opportunities at local and industry events. These led to invitations to participate in policy discussions at the state and national levels and to testify before the U.S. Senate on workforce issues. Soon other companies agreed to recruit candidates from the PowerPathway program. What began as a way to help PG&E overcome its challenges as baby boomers retired—her first drop in the pond—grew into significant improvements across the entire utility industry.

Within four years, the Obama administration recognized PG&E for its workforce efforts, and more companies began to adopt the PowerPathway model. This led to Ton-Quinlivan's appointment by Governor Jerry Brown to lead workforce and economic development at the statewide level as vice chancellor of the California Community College System. This allowed her to parlay her experiences into a larger platform—to impact more students and improve the systems that serve them. She now has opportunities to broaden her reach across a much larger pond.[3]

Ton-Quinlivan would certainly tell you that having the initial idea for PowerPathway was not enough. It was only when she brought together the many recommendations and aligned to the disparate interests of internal and external stakeholders that she made the program a success. She had to have dozens and dozens of conversations over many months in order to bring her stakeholders on board and assemble the bricolage of their ideas into what was eventually a successful model. She always pushed herself to stay open to new ways of thinking rather than believing that her ideas were the only good ones. *What can you do today to build on your ideas by learning from and aligning to others' interests?*

Nurture Divergent and Consilient Thinking

For Van Ton-Quinlivan at PG&E and Jennifer Gill Roberts at FWE, doing business as usual was no longer an option. Not only could they clearly see the enormous challenges in their respective arenas, but it was also clear that "the way things have always been done" was no longer sufficient. The utility industry was undergoing enormous demographic shifts as thousands of longtime workers were set to retire. In the entrepreneurial world, as more and more women were starting companies, it was obvious to Roberts that with only 1 percent of the venture financing going to women-led companies, something needed to change.

To make a difference and address the long-term trends in your industry, you will likely find, as Roberts and Ton-Quinlivan did, that you need to find entirely new models or ways of approaching the problems or opportunities ahead. You'll have to push out of your normal boundaries and explore many different paths; nurture divergent thinking and consilient thinking, which Edward O. Wilson explains in his book *Consilience* as "the ability to link facts and fact-based theory across disciplines to create a common groundwork of explanation."[4]

How did Ton-Quinlivan practice divergent thinking? She brought a model and approach from the biotech industry into the utility industry and pushed people to try something that she had seen work elsewhere. How did she practice consilient thinking? She combined ideas from her research in educational reform and teaching in the community college system and then adapted and adopted the ideas of many different stakeholders to build a successful program. In Roberts's case, rather than follow the expected path of starting another investment fund to provide financing to a few more women entrepreneurs, she took a divergent path, creating FWE to address the underlying challenges faced by all women starting high-growth companies. This allowed her to have a much broader impact, and to scale her efforts far beyond the Bay Area.

The master of divergent and consilient thinking was Steve Jobs. He crossed many different boundaries: computers, animation, design, mobility. He took ideas from each area into the others. One small example: a calligraphy class he took in college led him to invest in creating the very beautiful fonts that were available on the first Macintosh computer. He understood that the ease with which he crossed boundaries helped him to stand out from others around him. "A lot of people in our industry haven't had very diverse experiences. So they don't have enough dots to connect, and they end up with very linear solutions without a broad perspective on the problem. The broader one's understanding of the human experience, the better design we will have."[5]

Look for new ideas from fields that regularly overlap with yours—or that are completely orthogonal. Go far beyond the normal boundaries to places others don't think about, have experience in, or even recognize as places to seek new ways of thinking. Find opportunities to explore completely new fields. The fact that I have worked in the travel, legal, technology, medical device, and utility industries, as well as in politics, education, entrepreneurship, and women's leadership, means I have a wide variety of perspectives and that allows me to draw connections far outside the norm.

CASE STUDY: STEVE CRAFT

One person who understands the importance of broadening access to new ideas is Steve Craft. In 2009, Craft was the deputy director in the Strategic Relationships Office at the NASA Langley Research

Center. As such, he had a front-row seat to the changes under way at the space agency. He was well aware that the world as they knew it was about to undergo a significant transformation. NASA's funding for manned spaceflight had been cut, and within a few years the space shuttle program, which had already been extended well beyond original design goals, would no longer be one of their primary missions.

Craft had been looking for ways to get the word out about the other scientific accomplishments and amazing talent of the NASA community. He also hoped to "wake up the creativity and innovation again." He knew that NASA had a lot of "exceptionally smart people and they'd been doing really great things for a long time," but to Craft it appeared "they were hibernating."[6] Thus, when the opportunity came his way to host an in-house TEDx (Technology, Entertainment & Design, x = independently organized) Conference at NASA, he jumped at the chance.[7]

He wondered, "What if I could cross-pollinate the brilliance of the NASA community with new ideas from the outside? What if I could broaden the challenges that NASA scientists are tackling—to create opportunities for our engineers and scientists to not only solve the challenges of space but also solve other of the world's tough problems?"

He told me, "TED is all about people from all walks of life presenting talks about really big challenges—and one of NASA's biggest strengths is solving tough problems. Let's put them together and see what happens." What happened was that Craft's first event, which he brought together with little support and almost no budget in only a few months, attracted not 100 people, as the TED organizers had expected, but over 1,500 attendees in person and over 77,000 people from ten countries live online.

It also caused some unexpected outcomes. The NASA attendees definitely "woke up their creativity." One of the scientists, who had been doing research on how to decrease the vibrations that happen when rockets take off, began to think in new ways—inspired by new techniques he learned while teaching himself to play the piano at home. His breakthrough solution utilized thinking both from the left (more analytical) side of the brain and the right (more creative) side, something Craft had introduced at TEDxNASA. In addition, the people who lived near NASA Langley learned about their neighbor for the first time. As one attendee told Craft, "You know, I've been here twenty years and I've learned more about NASA in one day than I've learned in all of those twenty years combined."

Over the next two years, TEDxNASA events spread to two other NASA centers and sparked interest in all ten. Three TEDx Youth@NASA events were also held, opening the world of NASA's ideas to the next generation. What started as a skunkworks[8] effort by Craft to nurture new thinking among company employees also led to many new engaging outreach events with entities like NASCAR and Busch Gardens. Craft is now using his strategic insights to help craft a thirty-year vision for NASA in the newly established ReVITALization Office at NASA Langley.

What can you do today to nurture divergent and consilient thinking?

Here are a few approaches:

- Build connections with industry analysts, pundits, or journalists who can serve as a source of new ideas and a way to test your own.
- Join academic conference committees, advisory groups, or university research teams.
- Serve on the boards of professional, regional, or industry organizations.
- Start or join LinkedIn groups or Meetups or Facebook communities in your niche; volunteer to serve as a curator of information for the group.
- Seek appointments to government bodies, policy groups, or award committees where you'll have broad access to a wide network of ideas.
- Read widely, take a class, study big thinkers like Thomas Edison (try the great book *Innovate Like Edison*,[9] which shares his five competencies of innovators).

- Attend a conference completely outside your industry; watch a TED Talk or an Ignite Talk on YouTube.
- Expand your TV watching from evening dramas and the news to include biographies of great innovators or even *Shark Tank* or *The Pitch*. Or read the biography of a successful CEO.

FIND YOUR STAKEHOLDERS

We have discussed the importance of sharing your *What If?* future with lots of different people, but how do you know who the right people are? At this stage you are looking for strategic stakeholders, those who owe you loyalty equity, and even those who are eager to disagree with you.

Start with Your Strategic Stakeholders

It may surprise you to learn that at this stage you are not necessarily looking for people who will help you implement your ideas (although if you do find some, that would be great). Instead you need people who can validate, add to, modify, confirm, build on, or align with any efforts you might have under way. You want to share your WIF with people who are more informed than you are about your arena, but also those who have a stake in seeing you succeed.

For Van Ton-Quinlivan, the first step to catalyze her Power-Pathway efforts was to identify potential strategic stakeholders both inside and outside her company. She needed people she could toss ideas around with, who had some "skin in the game," or who were willing to help her because they knew and trusted her.

Think of your strategic stakeholders as the people with the keys to those doors leading from the room you are standing in today to new adjacent possible futures. They may not be in those adjacent rooms themselves, but they may have a connection to someone who could open new doors. You're looking for people you know who can help you flesh out your ideas and turn them into workable solutions. Those who are the potential beneficiaries of your activities are most likely to help out. Look for people with positions of influence and those Malcolm Gladwell calls the Connectors[10]—those who know everyone.

The unfortunate thing about this process is that you don't always know who is holding a key to your adjacent possible. Toni Quinlivan began with the people whose jobs would be or could be affected by the new programs she wanted to institute. But then she had to go broader and deeper, both inside and outside her company. As she put together the framework of what she wanted to accomplish, she had to find the right people who would and could help her bring about the first ripples of change.

She didn't start out knowing that she was going to create PowerPathway; she started out looking for a possible solution to several big, intractable problems. She began her discussions with her own small team, then with her colleagues, her mentor, an outside consultant (me), her internal sponsors, people she had served with on a local board, and others she had met and trusted in her industry.[11] Not only did everyone give her advice and counsel, but many also joined her team to make the first PowerPathway program a success.

Who holds the keys to your adjacent possible? Who might give you advice, and who might join your "team"?

Consider these ideas:

- Always start by reaching out to your personal board of directors (see more about this in Chapter Four).
- If you are creating a new initiative internally, look for people from other departments or divisions, or individuals who are most likely to be impacted by your activities.
- If you work in a community role, look for policy makers, board members, or legislators who are focused on the same goals.
- If you work in a nonprofit, think of clients your nonprofit has served, donors who have supported you, or volunteers and staff members who can weigh in or help you get under way.
- If you're a technology entrepreneur, look for engineers or experts from your technical arena or a related field.

- You can also look to the members of a group you belong to, online or off. This can be any supportive group where confidentiality is guaranteed.

Those who can open the doors to our adjacent possible can be anywhere; they could even be sitting in the next cubicle. Any number of conversations can hold the keys to new ideas that may alter your perspective as well as new connections that could help you get an initiative under way. *Who are your strategic stakeholders?*

Who Owes You Loyalty Equity?

When Steve Craft began his TEDxNASA journey, he had neither a team nor an existing community who saw him as their natural leader. In fact, his own boss told him not to spend time on starting up an event but to stay focused on the goals they'd originally set for the year. He had to begin at the beginning: bringing people on board one by one. I asked Craft to explain his success, and he replied, "Primarily it was the 'loyalty equity' that I had built up over the years I had been with the organization.

"Most of the people that I needed to bring together to make TEDxNASA happen had never been to a TED conference. In 2009, the TED videos were online but hadn't become very popular yet. This vision of what it could mean to bring TED and NASA together—others really didn't see that. But what I had was loyalty equity—the people who worked with me before or knew me at NASA knew that I had a good reputation, knew that I had good character, knew that I could make things happen. They were excited to work with me, no matter what. And even though they couldn't really be sure what I was doing, they were like, 'Well, if Steve is doing it, I'm doing it.'

"So, that carried me through the first one. By the second year, we had all the folks on board that had been to the first one, and we could show other people the video we had put together when we were trying to explain what TEDxNASA was. Many more people wanted to be involved the second year. But that first year, I could not have made it happen without the loyalty equity that I had built up from my many years at NASA."[12] *Who owes you loyalty equity? How are you building loyalty equity now so you have it "in the bank" to use later?*

Who Disagrees with You?

It may seem counterintuitive, but many times the best people to talk with at this stage are not exclusively those who have a vested interest in your success. You also want to hear from those who would prefer that you don't succeed. Yes, I'm really serious.

When you face the challengers, the naysayers, the Eeyores (those who never think anything good will possibly happen), you will gain a crucial understanding of what you might be up against. It's not possible (at least most of the time) to bring everyone on board with a new idea immediately. Overlooking those who stand in your way or are adverse to your ideas means you won't know all of the objections you may need to overcome. Hear from the naysayers early because they can lead you in a new direction and help frame which path you take.

George Eliot said, "Every limit is a beginning as well as an ending." By hearing from the naysayers, you learn the limits early—you identify which doors are presently closed to you—so you can find a workaround or rethink your path, or maybe learn why you never needed to go through that door to begin with! Besides, winning someone over who was initially not on your side can be very rewarding and often these folks can be your staunchest supporters, once you've overcome their initial objections.

But take a little advice here from Sara Blakely, CEO of SPANX (who turned five thousand dollars into a billion dollar undergarment company): please don't look for validation for your ideas exclusively from a family member or a really close friend. They are often too protective and may discourage you from taking a risk in case it doesn't work out and they are left to pick up the pieces.[13] Steve Craft's wife, Hayley Foster, became one of his biggest allies, but this is not always the case. If you don't get initial support at home, don't be deterred.

Here's a process that can help you manage your search for individuals and groups who might align with or oppose your efforts. For more ideas about how to find feedback on your ideas, see "More Food for Thought" at the end of the chapter.

1. Make a spreadsheet of all the potential strategic stakeholders you've identified. Think broadly about whom you have easy access to and people who might be harder to reach. Include them all on the list.
2. If you've already been spreading the word about your ideas, add those who have already shown an interest whom you can count as allies.
3. Add the "Connectors"—those people who are well networked and who might lead you to others.
4. Prioritize the list based on whom you know best and who are most likely to align with your ideas—or at least offer encouragement.
5. Take the prioritized list to a mentor, sponsor, or a member of your personal board of directors (see Chapter Four). Get their input on which individuals to approach first, who might find it easier to adapt to new ideas, as well as who might stand in your way. Ask for introductions to people on your list that they know.
6. Compile a list of questions you need to know the answers to before you can move forward. You won't ask every person you meet with the same set of questions, but don't hesitate to check the answers you hear from one stakeholder with another—this is where the real richness can unfold.
7. As you connect to each person on your spreadsheet, track whether or not they're willing to align with your interests. For those who are, keep them informed as you progress. (People always seem to forget this step!) They will often lead you to others if they remain in your "inner circle."

8. Think through what tasks you need help with so you can also engage people who are ready to jump on your bandwagon.

IT'S ABOUT THEM

Throughout this chapter I have urged you to have meetings with people who matter—people who can weigh in on your ideas. So it would be remiss of me not to spend a minute on the rules of the road when it comes to the etiquette of meetings. You may believe otherwise, but having been on the other side of the table from a lot of gung ho entrepreneurs and even experienced executives with a new idea, I can attest that you may be so fired up by what you want to say that you forget some simple courtesies.

Starting out, you may think people should listen to you because you are the expert—and you may well be. But people don't like to listen to experts; they like to *be* the expert. As a thought leader, your task is to build followers and evangelists and your goal is to catalyze others to take action. Dazzling someone with your amazing brilliance is not a successful strategy. People have to care about your message, then align themselves to your ideas, and finally spread that message to others. And that begins when you honor their intelligence and expertise and work to integrate their ideas into yours. The best way to do that is to *listen* to what they have to say.

As you prepare for a meeting, think through how you can craft a "why to buy" message that both encompasses what people believe today *and* prompts them to think in new ways. How will you align them with your way of thinking? We'll talk more about this in other chapters, but as you consider sharing your nascent idea, you have to remember:

It's not about you, it's about them.

Think about it from their perspective. Why should they jump on your bandwagon? What are the two or three key takeaways you want them to remember after the meeting? How can you organize the meeting to ensure that these messages are clearly communicated and remembered? Before you leave a meeting, have you created value for the person you've been meeting with? Have you created a peer-to-peer relationship so that the next time you call, they will pick up the phone?

Warm and friendly *and* well prepared is the winning combination. Share the personal story behind what you're committed to—that is far more likely to get people interested and excited by what you're doing. We all want to help people achieve something they are truly committed to.

If you can stand back and do a dispassionate analysis at each stage of your journey, you are likely to go far. Don't take it personally when people don't immediately align with the new ideas you are proposing. After each meeting, reflect on these questions:

- What were they willing to "buy"? What messages seemed to have heads nodding in agreement?
- What ideas did they have that broadened your thinking or took you in a new direction?
- Did you articulate your ideas in such a way that they were engaged? Do you need to strengthen or customize your message before you have additional meetings? (See the next chapter for how to prepare a message template.)
- What questions did they ask that you weren't prepared for? Can you send a follow-up email that addresses those questions?

After the meeting, complete any follow-up you committed to. The more often your *say:do* ratio is one to one (when you say you'll do something, you actually do it), the more likely you'll build support. And perhaps most important, *say thank you*—early and often.

DON'T GIVE UP TOO EASILY

Often, when you start out, you have a small idea, and you engage with stakeholders in order to build it into a much bigger idea. But what if you already have a big idea and it terrifies you? Or what if you're not sure whether you're the right person to move it forward? This is when it's critical to let the "market" decide, use zero-based thinking, and let go of perfection.

Let the "Market" Decide

A friend of mine, a professional consultant, told me that the previous year she had conceived of the idea of convening a conference for senior executives from all of the companies in her professional expertise. She came home all excited, but even as she began to explain to her husband what she was thinking she stopped herself and said, "I can't put a conference together." And that was that.

Reflecting on it, she told me she didn't even perceive any lack of support from him; it was her own fear of taking on something she had never done before that held her back. Others in her industry are now hosting similar events to what she'd envisioned, and she is kicking herself for stepping away from her own idea without having taken the time to determine if it was feasible.

We all have similar stories of ideas we abandoned too soon. The advice I give my clients (and myself) is that rather than discard an untested idea (particularly a big idea), we should let the "market" decide. If you get out and talk to people and start to hear that what you're contemplating has others excited, you are likely on the right track. Then your role is to identify others who can help you make it happen (as we'll discuss more in the next chapter).

However, if you are not getting any traction for your idea, how do you know when to give up? I believe we can learn something from the best inventors and entrepreneurs: iterate, hone, and modify. Great inventors tinker and adapt and are not afraid to test their own assumptions or redo things that aren't working.

Transportation entrepreneur Robin Chase, the founder and former CEO of the car-sharing company Zipcar, advises that you think of everyone you test your ideas on as a free consultant. When they ask you a question, don't think, "Aren't they stupid because they don't get it." Think instead, "Aren't I stupid because

I can't explain this so they can understand it." She advises that you carefully collect the questions and objections you hear so that you can learn what *will* sell your idea. Hone and modify and learn how to express things in a way that others will both understand and get excited. That's when you know you can move forward.[14]

How will you listen for what others respond to (and learn what doesn't) and make modifications accordingly? If you need more suggestions for how to test your ideas, see "More Food for Thought" at the end of the chapter.

Use Zero-Based Thinking

Often you come to a crossroads: you've been testing and iterating for a while, but nothing seems to be the idea that "sticks." When you reach that point, remember one important truism I learned in business school: *sunk costs are sunk.* This means that even if you've sunk a lot of money into a project, that is still not a good enough reason to keep going forward.

No matter how much time and energy and political capital (or money) you've already invested in an idea, don't let that be the reason you keep going. You can't recover the time and money you've already spent, and there is no point in expending more. Instead, stop and practice zero-based thinking: re-look, re-think, re-assess what you're doing with fresh eyes.

Ask yourself these questions:

- Is the path that I'm on now the one that I'd be on if I were starting this effort today?
- If I were to start right now, from where I stand today, would I be focused on the activities that I've been spending my time on?
- Am I throwing good money (resources, time, energy, people) after bad because I'm unwilling to stop and admit I'm going down the wrong path?
- Are there any signals that show me that I'm going in the right direction?

- Can I identify three things that need to happen in the next month (or quarter or year) that will assure me I'm on the right path? If I don't achieve those milestones, can I commit to stop what I'm doing and try something completely new?

Done—Not Perfect

Sheryl Sandberg, author of the bestseller *Lean In* and the COO of Facebook, argues, "Done is better than perfect."[15] I couldn't agree more. Always seeking perfection in thought leadership may be counterproductive. Holding out for every single possible nuance of risk to be worked out before you move forward is a recipe for disaster. To avoid analysis-paralysis, align with a friend or colleague who can ensure that you test your ideas adequately without taking yourself out of the game. Then assume that the only way to find success is to have some failure along the way. Celebrate it! It's called learning. *How can you let good enough BE good enough?*

Once you've tested, iterated, and validated your kernel of a transformative idea and molded it into a workable idea that has gained some early supporters, it's time to think about how you'll go from initial ripples in the pond to a broader initiative for change. Now you need to broaden your message beyond the early stakeholders to engage with people you don't know and who don't know you, those with the clout and connections to take you much further. That's what we'll cover in the next chapter.

BUILD YOUR RIPPLES OF INFLUENCE: A QUICK REVIEW

In this step of the thought leadership journey, successful thought leaders

- Begin to expand their "adjacent possible" by sharing their *What If?* future with friends and colleagues to learn what resonates

- Are open to adapting an outside idea from another industry or market sector. They use divergent and consilient thinking to assemble a bricolage of existing ideas into a new path they will explore
- Identify their strategic stakeholders, including those who owe them "loyalty equity," who can open more doors to a new adjacent possible
- Face the naysayers in order to make sure that an audience or group of individuals exists that is interested in the same WIF they are committed to bring about
- Create conversations that are not only "selling" their own idea to others but learning from and incorporating potential stakeholders' ideas into their own
- Continually adapt, modify, and redesign their program, project, or process along the way to bring in multiple viewpoints and recommendations
- Use zero-based thinking to regularly reassess that they are going in the right direction and let go of perfection

---

MORE FOOD FOR THOUGHT

Find Additional Feedback

One of the wonderful things about new ideas is that there are always a lot of people who are willing to weigh in with their thoughts, caveats, issues, and concerns—as well as their suggestions, recommendations, and modifications. Here are a few more ideas on how to get feedback on a new idea.

Ask your followers: If you already have a responsive following—an email list or people following your blog—try writing a short, provocative piece spelling out what you're thinking and encourage people to comment or write you

(*continued*)

back. Or send out a survey using an online survey tool. You'll quickly discover which people might be worth following up with, and you'll also learn the common questions or concerns that arise when people hear about this new idea.

Host a listening tour: Just as politicians "go on the road" to hear from their constituencies, can you identify communities that might have an interest in your ideas or whom you need to hear from? Scan your contact list to develop an invite list to a series of meetings with different communities or jointly host the tour with a prominent industry leader or trade association. When Van Ton-Quinlivan wanted to introduce a new framework to community college stakeholders, she made herself available to speak at their local town-hall meetings which brought together business and workforce development leaders as well as educators. These forums gave her the opportunity to share her plans as well as hear from those who would be most affected.

Pretotype and prototype: Often what is most challenging in trying to engage people with your ideas is getting them to "see" the future as you do. In the technology arena, two concepts have helped product teams gain the necessary feedback before making a large investment: pretotyping and prototyping. You are probably familiar with prototyping—creating a working model of a proposed product quickly and inexpensively, to find out if there is a market need. A "pretotype" is the step before the prototype. When Jeff Hawkins was developing the Palm Pilot—the first successful personal digital assistant—he began by cutting out a block of wood and adding a piece of paper on one side that delineated the possible placement of the screen and the buttons. He walked around for months carrying this mock-up in his pocket, pulling it out experimentally to determine whether he would actually use a device like this, and iterating it until he had the feel exactly right. This block of wood was his pretotype and gave him all the feedback he needed to make certain that when the first prototype was actually built it would not be a waste of money.[16] Could you pretotype or prototype your ideas? Would a video animation, using a tool like Videoscribe,[17] help others understand what you've imagined?

Crowdsource: Send out an open call for solutions to a wide variety of networks. Outline what you're looking for and offer a prize to recognize those whose solutions are adopted. In May 2013, eight different organizations formed the Global Women's Leadership Alliance and offered a $1,000 prize for ideas on how to radically accelerate the development of leadership capacity in women and girls around the globe.[18] In March 2013, the Gates Foundation put out a call to action offering a $100,000 start-up grant to the person who designs "the next generation condom."[19]

Convene: Early in my book-writing process, I convened groups of friends to discuss topics I was considering including. Their ideas added to the richness of each chapter and helped me hone my thinking. I also got wonderful input when I convened editing parties and asked my friends for advice as the book was under way.

Use participatory design: Actively involve all the stakeholders (employees, partners, customers, citizens, end users) in the design process through focus groups, brainstorming sessions, and so on. When author and social entrepreneur Miki

(continued)

Agrawal began to explore starting a healthy pizza restaurant at the age of twenty-five, she had no industry experience, but she did have a wide and varied network.

She convened about twenty people she knew, including bankers, interior designers, and an architect, for dinner and brainstorming, and in a few hours they put together her menu and came up with a clever name, Slice Perfect, for her first restaurant. The many other ideas they developed that night ensured that her New York City restaurant (later renamed Wild, http://eatdrinkwild.com) rose above the rest. She told me that it was the variety of contradictory opinions that gave her the confidence that she would meet the expectations of the widest possible audience.

Agrawal went on to open a second restaurant and gain adoption for her locally sourced and healthy pizza among schools, hotels, and restaurants. This attracted the attention of Tony Hsieh of Zappos, who funded her to open a 110-seat restaurant in downtown Las Vegas. She then founded a social venture, THINX, using many of the ideas she had learned along the way. Agrawal has since documented her adventures in her book *Do Cool Sh*t*.[20]

What are some creative ways you can get feedback for your ideas?

CHAPTER 3

ACTIVATE YOUR ADVOCATES

In the last chapter, we talked about what it takes to make the first ripples in your pond—testing and iterating an idea and gaining initial buy-in. But bringing about a big *What If?* future requires going beyond one program, one initiative, or one small team. It requires multiplying your initial ripples of influence to create not only incremental modifications around the edges but a much needed shift in the status quo. To do this you will need to enlist a much broader set of champions and allies who can adopt your ideas and advocate or evangelize on behalf of your efforts, or even lead initiatives that mirror the ones you've begun.

How do you find these people? How do you help them see why they should get on board? What preparation do you need in order to engage and motivate them? How do you make it not solely your idea or project or program but also theirs? These are the challenges (and opportunities) we will address in this chapter. One of the people who successfully engaged a wide network of advocates in support of her WIF was Mary Hughes of the 2012 Project. In so doing, she not only created momentum around her ideas; she also had a far-reaching impact on local, state, and federal elections across the United States.

CASE STUDY: MARY HUGHES AND THE 2012 PROJECT

In 2006, when Mary Hughes was invited to participate in a retreat about women's political participation at the Center for American Women and Politics (CAWP) at Rutgers University, she had no idea that this meeting was the beginning of a personal journey. That journey would not only catapult her to the national stage, having a significant impact on the 2012 election, but also require her to rethink, diversify, and expand her network of advocates and associates acquired over twenty-five years.

Mary Hughes is a longtime political consultant whose client list reads like the who's who of California politics. She has dedicated her career to advising progressive candidates in local, state, and federal races and is well known in the halls of power from Los Angeles to Sacramento.

The CAWP retreat was focused on the ongoing underrepresentation of women in state legislatures and Congress. Hughes knew that women's representation in Congress was stagnant at 16 percent with only two or three additional women elected to Congress each cycle. Women's representation in state legislatures had crawled from 20 to 22 percent over the previous decade. Things were not getting better; indeed women's political leadership had flatlined. The attending scholars, donors, and political operatives spent hours discussing needed research that the center might do to better understand why there was so little progress.

Hughes came away from the full day of conversation thinking, "This has gone on long enough." She wondered, "What strategy could we use to fundamentally change the circumstances as they exist today?" In the face of women losing ground or making small, incremental gains in each election, she wondered how to bring about significant increases in the number of women in Congress and state legislatures.

Over the next two years, she spent time researching that question, examining the factors from 1992, the last time women's representation had increased significantly. She canvassed the people in her political circle, authored a white paper, and began to share it, refining her thinking as she gained more input from people she respected. Following the 2008 election, when it was clear that little had changed, she decided to throw herself into the issue full-time.

As she researched recent election data and tested her ideas with colleagues, Hughes came to realize that 2012 would offer a rare opportunity for women candidates. The confluence, which happened only once every twenty years, of a presidential election (which brought many more people to the polls) and political reapportionment and redistricting (a once-a-decade event when many new seats opened up), would give women many more opportunities to break into politics for the first time. She also discovered that while there are groups focused on supporting women candidates, there were very few organizations actively recruiting women to run for office. The research findings were clear: women were more likely to run if they were asked, and women won at the same rate as men. The problem was simply that far fewer women were running. She decided that recruitment was the weak link, and that would be the niche she would stake out.

Hughes wanted to learn how to identify, engage, and motivate women to run for office for the first time—not just for city council and school board seats but for state legislatures and Congress. Her strategy was to do "direct outreach to executive-level, accomplished women, particularly women of color, in the private and public sectors who had not previously considered running for office." She would enlist the help of former elected women to make the case at annual conventions, professional association meetings, and monthly luncheons that public service was rewarding and productive and that women could make a difference.

If women were interested in running for office, they would be connected with the many resources in their communities that could teach them how to campaign and support their candidacies. Simultaneously, she would mobilize statewide coalitions of women's organizations to spread the word and launch a large-scale public education campaign to raise awareness of the issue.

As a result of her research, Hughes also came to realize that staying firmly entrenched on one side of the political aisle was not a winning strategy for recruiting among women with no prior political involvement. She recognized that she must create a national, nonpartisan effort—one that would allow women to consider running without first coming face to face with partisan polarization. Introducing the subject from a nonpartisan platform made sense.

"For twenty-five to thirty years, I had worked exclusively with Democratic candidates," Hughes told me, so a nonpartisan initiative "was a hard thing for me to come to grips with. One piece of research that I really appreciated was that one of the reasons women are not motivated to run for office (in fact, they are put off politics and elections) is the hardline partisanship and the negativity. It seemed that if you want more women to run—if you're going to ask more women to run—maybe you should approach them from the civic activism angle, good government, and leave party aside for that initial contact. That turned out to be a good instinct, I think."

Going this route required her to set aside partisanship and think, "Women first," a choice many of her longtime political allies were not interested in making. "I had said I wanted to experiment, to come at problems differently. There I was doing it differently, but many of my allies weren't there—some were, but most weren't. When I realized that I was entering a whole new realm beyond my normal Democratic political network, then I had to say, 'Make it an adventure.'"

Without her traditional base of longtime political allies and organizations, Hughes explained, "I didn't really know how to begin." To find sponsors and partners she had to "create new alliances, build bridges to communities outside of political activist women." She had to "find people who believed in this and who were persuaded by the need for more women in office and willing to take a risk."

To be effective, she recognized that she would need a strong, national partner with an established brand and connections. In 2009, looking for input and potential partners, she sent the white paper about her initiative, now entitled the 2012 Project, to foundations and institutes, and she quickly learned that several were eager to join forces.

Conversations with the CAWP at Rutgers University, which had hosted the retreat that had sparked her interest initially, led her to decide to take the campaign there. The CAWP was considered the gold standard of research on women and elections, and Hughes liked the idea of anchor teams on both coasts; but more importantly, the CAWP already had leadership programs in place on college campuses throughout the country. It also had an extended network of bipartisan contacts in the national women's community and would provide the financial and administrative component that a lean team could not. The staff shared her mission, and they were fun to collaborate with.

Once she had this institutional weight on the ground, they recruited a top-notch team with extensive campaign experience and built a bipartisan "faculty" of seventy former elected women from both political parties who would spread the message of the 2012 Project. As Hughes explained, "When Jo Ann Davidson, the former cochair of the Republican National Committee and the first woman speaker of the Ohio House of Representatives, and Connie Morella, a former Republican member of Congress from Maryland, joined Democrats, including former Vermont governor Madeleine Kunin, former California congresswoman Yvonne

Burke, and former Colorado State Senator Polly Baca to cochair the 2012 Project faculty, it was clear that a different approach was really possible. Those were the early wins in expanding our reach that let me see that the nonpartisan nature of our message was going to get us where we needed to go."

And go they did. While Hughes is modest about taking credit for the success of women candidates in the 2012 election cycle, she credits the 2012 Project with engaging over five hundred women from the private sector and providing them with road maps to explore a run for office. They also connected these potential candidates with campaign boot camps, fundraising trainings, leadership institutes, and think tanks. Of these 500 potential candidates, 129 filed to run for office and 30 were successful. Another 56 were prepared to run in the next two elections.

Hughes's 2012 Project had much broader consequences than those for individual candidates. It brought significant new resources, awareness, and momentum to their political organization partners and to the much broader efforts under way. "The entire enterprise [of bringing more women into the political landscape] was lifted up by the collective efforts of so many women who made this their priority in 2012, and we were a part of that."[1]

Early in her career, Mary Hughes found the *What If?* future she was committed to bring about—more Democratic women candidates *elected* to political office—and she dedicated her career to that goal. Yet after twenty-five years she realized that the opportunities for women had not improved in any meaningful way despite her best efforts. To increase her impact on the political landscape, she needed to redirect her efforts to the challenge of getting more women to *run* for office. That required a widespread invitation and a message that women's experiences and perspectives are unique and valuable, and that their presence in office matters.

I often encounter this moment with my clients: the day they wake up and think, "Is this enough?" Often they have spent many years working in one company or making incremental progress on one issue, and they have seen some improvements due to their efforts. But then they look up and realize that there is much more they want to accomplish in their careers and much more that needs to be done to achieve the broader *What If?* future they envision. At that point, it becomes critical that they identify supporters who can take them to the next level and give them access to a broader stage.

IDENTIFY POTENTIAL SUPPORTERS

Many change agents find that their initial efforts to push a new idea or program forward can be done as volunteer projects—with friends and borrowed resources and a lot of hard work. That was certainly how we started FWE and the Springboard venture conference and how others mentioned in this book got under way. But once those initial efforts show some success, it is time to get serious about finding a way to expand the number of people engaged with what you're doing. To really push forward a big *What If?* future, you must identify people who are willing and able to help you accomplish scale.

If you're lucky, you have an existing team or a budget to hire people. But often you don't have that luxury—or, like Mary Hughes, you find that your initial network is not aligned to your new direction. Then you have to get much more creative in identifying champions and allies who will join your efforts.

The good news? If you have crafted a compelling *What If?* future, others out there will be eager to help. Your "job" is to find them and then attract them, engage them, and invite them to join you.

Champions and Allies

A quick definition of terms here. *Champions* are people who will put their reputation on the line for you and your efforts. They are willing to pick up the phone, make an introduction, or speak publicly on your behalf. They align their reputation with yours, and by doing so they move your efforts forward substantially. *Allies* are people who are ready and willing to roll up their sleeves and do the heavy lifting.

They will not only give you their advice; they will put in time, money, and elbow grease to actually push for real transformative change. (Yes, some people might be both allies and champions!)

Here's where to look for champions:

- Leaders in other departments, divisions, or companies that face the same challenges
- Community leaders or industry spokespeople who champion the same ideas
- Researchers who have been studying the issues that you care about
- Analysts who issue reports in your industry niche
- Journalists who write frequently about what you are interested in
- Foundation, institutional, or government officials whose organizations fund, study, or regulate the same issues
- Officials in regulatory bodies or trade associations that oversee activities in your arena
- Pundits others refer to as the go-to people in your niche or an adjacent niche

Here's where to look for potential allies:

- People who share your job title in other departments or divisions in your company
- People in your industry (outside your company) who share the same job title or job responsibilities that you do
- Employees or former employees; colleagues or former colleagues
- Members of an online forum in which you're involved
- Members of nonprofits, regional organizations, trade associations, or political groups that are aligned to your ideas
- People you know, even peripherally, who have time to give to something they believe in
- People you know who are great at getting things done—the busiest people are often the most willing to help

You won't necessarily enroll all of these people, but the potential is there. In seeking allies and champions, don't just share your ideas; ask for people's help and believe that others want to get on board. Lots of potential allies and champions are out there who already agree with your *What If?* future or have a vested interest in helping you bring it about.

Once I connected with the broader entrepreneurial ecosystem—which included the National Women's Business Council and the Kauffman Foundation—I went from CEO of a small nonprofit in the Bay Area to a central role in the broader, national women's entrepreneurship community. Not only did my efforts scale much more quickly; I began to learn about national activities in which my organization could play a part. It was exciting to realize that others saw an even bigger vision than I did—I simply had to figure out how our efforts fit together and then be sure to align my organization's efforts with theirs. The day I was invited to join a meeting at the White House of people from across the country who were focused on improving the opportunities for women entrepreneurs, I realized that what we were doing at FWE could have an impact far beyond our initial vision.

As you find and join the broader ecosystem, you'll need to make your own decisions about how you can add your ripples to others (or vice versa). It's up to you whether you will align your efforts through a loose array of informal personal contacts and jointly hosted events, as I did, or whether you'll structure a more formal partnering arrangement, like Mary Hughes's. Just remember, this is not all about you. You also need to be a valuable ally to others!

CONSIDER WHAT'S IN IT FOR THEM

What motivates others to join your efforts? Once you understand the range of reasons for which someone might be willing to join your camp, you can use that information to craft the right message for your audiences and create the "marketing" materials that speak to their concerns and desires. Addressing what's in it for them is an important part of your message.

Here are descriptions of some of the most common and powerful motivators, with reflection questions for you.

Altruism   Do not underestimate altruism—in this context, a desire to support an idea, program, or future we believe in, not for personal gain but for the greater good. Just as you have an interest in leaving a legacy that matters, many others are inspired to align with or support an idea or cause they believe in for altruistic reasons. I found a lot of people like this along my thought leadership journey. We had volunteers at FWE, like marketing maven Jill Rubin, who stayed actively involved for ten years, despite no pay and little recognition. They were there to make a difference—and they did!

How do you propose to the altruistically motivated that they join you? Sell them on the big vision, the *What If?* future that you will bring about with their help. How do you know when you've found altruism at work? When you find someone who hears your story and immediately wants to help without seeking anything for themselves. *To what altruistic tendencies could you appeal to get people on board with your efforts?*

Shared Point of View   Closely tied to the concept of altruism is the sense, for some, for how the world should be. They are willing to give their time, money, energy, and connections to something if you can assure them it will help bring about a much better future world, even if it takes years to accomplish. To attract these folks, you are selling hope—hope that that future is possible and they can be one of the game-changers who will help to bring it about. Mary Hughes found many people across the United States who shared her point of view that it was time for more women in public office. These allies were a big part of the reason for the success of the 2012 Project.[2]

Look for people who espouse a shared point of view—those who may know even more than you about what you're trying to achieve. In the early days of FWE, I found there were many people who were more knowledgeable about women's entrepreneurship than I was; some had been working in that arena for years. They were eager and excited by the initiative I had under way and more than ready to provide their help—connections, ideas, and volunteer hours. *How can you find others who are already aligned to the cause you have under way?*

Skill-Building   When Van Ton-Quinlivan was recruiting people from other departments to help her launch the Power-Pathway initiative at PG&E, she offered them a "development opportunity"—a chance to learn new skills and work with an entrepreneurial team within the company. Since she had only a small staff, she leveraged this little-used practice, which let her "borrow" employees from other parts of the company (usually part-time) to supplement her team. *What sort of learning opportunities can you offer others in relation to your project?*

Credibility and Reputation   In the early days of FWE, the first board members that my cofounder, Jennifer Gill Roberts, and I brought together were a big part of our organization's success. As we approached others to speak, become members, or join the board, they would look at the impressive list of women already involved and want "in" because of the credibility and reputation of those who were already with us. This was also true when we started the Springboard Venture Conference. Because Kay Koplovitz—a well-known and successful entrepreneur who was then on the board of Oracle—was involved, we gained supporters who wished to align to her as much as to the efforts we had under way. *Who can you get on board that would help you establish your credibility from the get-go?*

Social Capital   Closely tied to the issue of credibility is that of social capital: everyone wants to travel in the "right" circles, whatever they perceive those to be. They want the opportunity to meet other innovative thinkers or those willing to engage in a project or program they care about. If affiliating with your initiative will bring them into the circles they want to travel in, people are more likely to join you.

This doesn't mean you need to revise anything that you're doing—you don't *need* to engage people, organizations, or companies that are wealthy, well known, or well connected simply because they might attract others to get on board. But why not make your road easier? Their good connections can have a big impact, moving you into the fast lane. We can all think of at least one example of a single celebrity or noteworthy person who pushed a worthy cause into the spotlight. *How could you build your cachet in order to attract followers?*

Innovation   There is no question that some people are early adopters: they will get involved in whatever is new and potentially the next big thing. I'm certainly one of those people. I love the new, the *wow!* ideas, and the leaders who are setting out to improve the way things have always been done. To attract people like me, it's pretty critical to present the *big* idea, the *What If?* future—as opposed to an incremental change—and explain how unlikely that change is to come about without their help.

Big companies or stodgy industries are also seeking game-changing initiatives that they can't develop themselves. One of my clients, Nina Nashif, who is the founder and CEO of Healthbox, a unique accelerator program for healthcare start-ups, discovered that the well-established healthcare companies were willing to put in significant funding as she scaled her program across the United States and Europe. By aligning with something innovative, they were seen as more innovative by their employees as well as by potential employees and partners. It was a win-win deal. The Healthbox accelerator needed the big companies' clout and access to their resources; the large healthcare companies needed access to the innovation of the start-ups Nashif and her team brought together.[3] *What is innovative or* wow! *about what you're doing? How can you let others—including early adopters and large entities in search of innovation—in on it?*

Media Attention   When you make a real difference in your city, community, or company, you will likely attract considerable media attention. It is good practice to not only use that attention to showcase your activities, but also to highlight the actions of your allies and partners, ensuring that they get their moment in the spotlight.

When FWE partnered with the National Women's Business Council and the Center for Women and Enterprise to launch the first Springboard Venture Conferences in three cities across the United States, we quickly had more press attention than we knew what to do with. The press loved writing stories featuring the seventy-five women entrepreneurs selected to present at our first three events. As part of our sponsorship packages for the events, we were able to offer our sponsors media attention—a chance to get their story out at the same time we were telling the Springboard story. We spotlighted their efforts as mentors to the Springboard participants, their role on our program committees, and their contributions of money, resources, and even our event venue.

The press attention that our sponsors received led to more people getting involved the second year. Using the press attention strategically to reward those who were involved helped us expand our efforts nationwide. *How could you use press attention to showcase your partners?*

Business Considerations   I began this section by talking about altruism and a shared point of view, but that doesn't mean that there may not be money in the equation somewhere. People will champion your efforts if you can help them figure out how they can make (or save) money or gain access to needed resources if they get involved. This doesn't have to be a quid pro quo (do this and you'll get that). There are far more subtle ways to make this connection for people. But don't hesitate to make it.

As we grew the membership of FWE, over time it became apparent to me that banks, law firms, and accounting firms wanted access to our members—women CEOs. They would write us a check, place a senior executive on our advisory board, or send a top leader to speak on a panel. We were happy to give them a chance to showcase their expertise to our members. If they did well, the women CEOs might hire their firm to provide needed services. It was a win-win situation.

When Mary Hughes sought out new partners to join the 2012 Project, she didn't go empty-handed. Her organization had access to needed resources, such as polling data, research on the right messages, and a top-notch faculty willing to speak at partners' events. None of these were easy to come by for small, regional non-profits. It didn't take them long to see the advantage of being part of her larger initiative. *How could people make money, find clients, or gain needed resources by aligning with what you have under way?*

DISCOVER WHAT MIGHT HOLD THEM BACK

When people evaluate a new idea, initiative, or project, there are many reasons they might want to get involved. But even when you come with your arms full of resources and have lots of innovative ideas, there will still be some people who won't join you. For Mary Hughes, this included those who weren't aligned with her bipartisan political message. For Van Ton-Quinlivan and Steve Craft, there were many nonbelievers who thought their efforts had little chance of success. Sadly, there are many reasons that hold people back from championing a new way of thinking.

Thus, in addition to determining what might attract potential allies to your ideas, part of your task is to give thought to what might preclude them from participating. As you are thinking about your potential supporters, what do you have to offer them and how will you reassure them that you are a valuable ally? The necessary trust can be built on a lot of different factors, especially:

Visibility: How visible is your initiative or project?

Credibility: Do you have any authority or standing in this arena? If not, are you aligned with any groups that have credibility?

Likeability and comfort level: How well do they know you? How much do they like you?

Reputation and reliability: How reliable and trustworthy have you been in the past? If you have allies who are part of the package you're presenting, what are their reputations for getting things done?

Brand: What is your brand, and what is the brand reputation of any organization you represent? Is it likeable, smart, and trustworthy, or are there issues you'll need to overcome? (Your brand reputation is related to many of the other items on this list. We'll discuss this more in later chapters.)

Baggage: Do you have any negatives—visible past problems, failures, gaffes—to overcome?

Confidence: Do you exude confidence in your ability to accomplish what's ahead? Are you fearless or timid? This can come across in myriad ways, from how you ask for what you need to your body language when you enter the room.

Sense of humor: Is there a sense of playfulness, humor, or fun in what you are proposing? Is it unusual, unique, or outside the box?

Loyalty: Have you shown loyalty to their ideas or initiatives? Do you have a track record of staying committed to projects over time?

Coachability: Are you willing to take advice or do you go it alone?

Network and trust circle: How broad is your network or community and how much does it overlap with theirs? Are you considered a "known" quantity? Do you have the support of others whom they are aligned with or who are supporting their efforts?

In my own experience, this last criterion has turned out to be one of the most important. I've always sought to build a broad network, but over time I have learned the importance of being on the inside of your potential supporter's trust circle. During the first year I worked full-time for the Forum for Women Entrepreneurs, I had just completed a pitch for sponsorship from a local bank and I was fairly sure it had gone well. I had spent hours preparing, and I'd done my homework on the organization. As I was leaving the room, one of the people who had attended the meeting said something to me that I've never forgotten. "That was a great pitch, Denise, but really, we are investing in you." Hmm.

At first I was flattered. *Wow, they're investing in* me! I thought. *I must have done a great job. They must really like me.* But as the months passed, I came to realize that it had more to do with the fact that they knew others in my trust circle. Many of my organization's members did their banking at that bank; we had a member of the bank's senior executive team on our board; and we were serving people who were right in the bank's "sweet spot"—entrepreneurs. The bank was willing to sponsor us because they wanted access to FWE members as potential banking clients.

Not only was what I was doing very visible to them, but also most of our programs were held in their backyard. They could easily communicate with everyone in my network. All of this combined meant that I was a part of their trust circle, and thus they could write me a check without a great deal of concern.

Often, ensuring that you build or establish trust and align others to your efforts depends more on some shared connection than on you individually. Use that connection to open the door for a meeting and then build trust from there.

Find links through these:

- A well-respected individual you both know
- A forum, organization, or affinity group where you are both members
- An alumni network

- A program or class in which you've both participated
- Membership in an online group with a shared interest
- An event you both attended

In the last few pages, we have discussed how to identify potential supporters and some reasons that they might or might not align with your ideas. Now it's time to take a few preparatory steps so that you are ready to head out into the world and find the allies and champions who will help you scale your efforts.

PREPARE TO SPAR

I have always liked the Henry Ford quote: "Before everything else, getting ready is the secret of success." In my work with clients, I recommend four important steps—most easily remembered with the acronym SPAR.

1. **S**et up tracking and connection tools
2. **P**repare a message template
3. **A**rticulate your plan of action
4. **R**ehearse, rehearse, rehearse

We'll go through each of these items one at a time in the pages that follow. But first, before you say, "Wait, this is too much work! I'm ready now," or "I'll figure it out as I go along," I assure you that the time and resources you invest to put these pieces in place will absolutely pay off. If you hone and clarify your message and develop a plan for where you're headed, you'll not only be ready; you'll know yourself to be ready. That confidence will all but guarantee your success.

Set Up Tracking and Connection Tools

Thought leaders have followers—hopefully, over time, lots of followers. When you're getting started, a simple spreadsheet works great (as we discussed in the last chapter) to track your initial stakeholders. Take the time to update that document regularly with additional potential allies and champions.

Add columns to the spreadsheet to track and prioritize those in your trust circle versus those in your network versus those you have heard about but don't yet know. Add a field for notes, where you can keep track of information you learn as you prepare for a meeting as well as follow up after you've connected with someone.

Van Ton-Quinlivan's PowerPathway team used their "Stakeholder Spreadsheet" for four years, updating it as more allies joined the efforts under way. At team meetings, the project manager used this spreadsheet as the basis for regular discussions about which allies might be willing to align to new team initiatives as well as which were likely to be naysayers.

Over time, as you continue to expand your reach, you will find that your spreadsheet is no longer sufficient for your purposes. I recommend identifying a database or CRM tool (try Salesforce.com or Contactually) that will allow you to track follow-up needed, what you learn in your meetings, information about their connections, and much more. You can segment your list and set reminders to reconnect with people over time.

Prepare a Message Template

Every (aspiring and experienced) thought leader has faced a moment when they didn't know what to say. And we've all walked away from an important interaction thinking, *Why didn't I remember to tell them about that important idea?* Without preparation, anyone may overlook even the most important point they meant to say. Or find they have so much to say that they can't stop talking.

I've learned to develop a message template, a one-page document that summarizes the key points that I want to say, as well as supporting data (proof points) and frequently asked questions and answers. Your message template is your talking-points document, and completing it will likely be the most valuable exercise you can do, bar none.

To get started, bring together three or four of the people who have been involved with your efforts to brainstorm your top three messages. (Following the template below, you'll focus on just three messages since that is the amount of information people can typically remember. And honing to three will force you to prioritize!) Then find someone who is a particularly good wordsmith to help you sharpen each point into memorable language.

The template prompts you to identify several "spoken messages," each based on "proof points." As you prepare your spoken messages, you are answering the question "What do my stakeholders/constituents need to hear/understand/learn in order to be on board with my idea/project/program?" Be sure you are writing from *their* perspective, not yours. Avoid jargon, acronyms, and any uncommon words or phrases that are not easily understood.

As you develop your proof points, you are answering the questions "What data or stories can I provide that prove my spoken message is true? Who is already aligned that proves my efforts are worth joining?"

To get started, focus on the items marked with "*" first.

* *Issue*: What is the core idea or issue you're focused on? What is your *What If?* future?

* *Summary*: Summarize the idea or issue in one sentence.

* *Objective*: Why are *you* trying to increase awareness of this idea or issue? What do you want to occur as a result of raising awareness?

Audience/Constituents: Who are your audiences or constituents?

Influencers: What stakeholders or constituencies influence your audience? Who has to be on board for your constituents to believe in or agree to align with your efforts?

What's in it for them: Why should your target audience get involved?

What holds them back: Why might they not get involved?

Channels: What internal and external channels are you going to use; for example, news media, speeches, testimony, customer and employee communications, publications, and events?

* *Unspoken message*: What are you trying to convey without saying it out loud? This is the hidden or underlying message in your communication that may not be as widely accepted if put in so many words. It may be the "not so politically correct" reason behind your actions or the not yet accepted truth that you believe but others do not.

* *Spoken message 1*: What is your first message (thought, idea, information), and what are the three proof points (research, data, past success) you have to clarify and verify what you are saying?

* *Spoken message 2*: What is your second message, and what are the three proof points you have to clarify and verify what you are saying?

* *Spoken message 3*: What is your third message, and what are the three proof points you have to clarify and verify what you are saying?

* *FAQ*: What questions are people likely to ask? What objections will they have to your ideas or point of view? What are the best responses to those questions?

* *Keywords*: What 5–10 keywords (#hashtags) best align with your message?

Do your best at drafting a good template even from the beginning, then update it regularly or when you sense the message needs revisiting—usually about every six months. Once your template is complete, you may not use every point in every meeting, but you will have identified the most relevant and compelling points to cover first. As your audiences vary, so will the items you choose to highlight. (Look for an example of a completed template in "More Food for Thought" at the end of this chapter.)

We'll talk more in later chapters about the importance of telling stories, but as you craft your message template, remember to share your personal background and why you are committed to the efforts you have under way. It never hurts to share your own hero's journey—the challenges you may have overcome to get to where you are today and your lessons learned along the way. The more you can encourage others to identify with you and your story, often the more likely they are to support your efforts.

Articulate Your Plan of Action

I am a big believer in planning—especially when the plan is short and to the point.

When I discovered Jim Horan's book *One Page Business Plan* in the library, I was an instant convert to his easy, template-driven system of planning, and I now use it with my clients.[4] You can quickly set measurable objectives, match strategies and action plans, and keep your goals front and center.

Your completed one-page action plan is also a very useful document to share with potential funders, champions, and team members so they can quickly align with your efforts. Use Horan's book (there's also one for nonprofits and for entrepreneurs) to develop your own plan, or hire a One Page Plan consultant in your area to help.[5]

The plan you write today will continue to evolve. If you don't have the full plan clearly in your mind, write down what feels possible today, then ask yourself, Is this far enough? What if I went even further? Who will support me and champion my efforts?

Rehearse, Rehearse, Rehearse

It doesn't matter how old or how experienced you are, a great presentation takes practice. Even Steve Jobs practiced for hours before going on stage. Conversely, former Nebraska Senator Charles "Chuck" Hegel failed to adequately prepare for his confirmation hearing for secretary of defense in 2013 and embarrassed both himself and the Obama administration. Think Steve, not Chuck!

You'll improve your chances enormously if you find someone to critique your presentation before you go live before an important stakeholder or audience. We'll talk about this more in the "Put Yourself on S.H.O.U.T." chapter; however, in addition to preparing what you want to say, you'll also need to prepare how to overcome objections and what to do when you get interruptions (as you will). Address objections with empathy and respect. Train yourself to answer the question, and then transition back to a key message on your message template.

What's your elevator speech—the fifteen-second encapsulated summary of your idea? I have sat through hundreds of pitches over the years, and they are consistently too long and far too detailed. I remember one call where someone pitched me for seventeen minutes without once stopping to find out if I was even on the phone any longer. (Yes, I timed her! And I didn't help her in the end. I had lost interest long before she stopped speaking.) The goal of any pitch is to get people to say "tell me more"—not to overwhelm them in the first few minutes with everything you know!

One other little trick: create a tie between what you're doing and something that your listener is familiar with. In Silicon Valley, I often hear companies pitch their ideas by saying something in the vein of, "We are creating the Yelp! for business software," or "We are the Pinterest for political information." Both of those descriptions immediately bring to mind big successes while simultaneously giving someone a shortcut to understand what you're doing. *How could you pitch your idea by tying it to something familiar?*

WHAT TO DO WHEN IT'S TIME TO ENGAGE

Now that you've gotten all of your materials prepared, let's think through what steps to take to move someone from initial interest to active involvement.

From Button to Billboard

One of the simplest techniques for engaging others is to ask for very little, at least at the start. You don't ask someone to marry you on the first date, do you? I learned a lot about the process of gaining incremental engagement the year I worked on a political campaign, supporting Steve Westly's candidacy for governor of California.

In my role as a campaign fundraiser, when I first met someone, my goal was to get them to write a small check and wear a campaign button for my candidate. Next I'd ask them to put a bumper sticker on their car and then a lawn sign in their front yard. At each stage, I hoped for a larger and larger investment in the candidate's success. Ultimately, what I really wanted was for them to write me a very large check and put a gigantic billboard on top of their house with my candidate's name prominently displayed in neon lights. (Okay, I might be exaggerating a little bit.)

Along with these outward signs of commitment, of course, I was hoping for an escalating commitment of time and connections. The very best outcome was for someone to be willing to host a large event and fill the room by evangelizing my candidate to their networks.

As you engage people with your activities, it's important to remember these steps—what I call the "Button to Billboard" engagement strategy. Start by asking for the equivalent of a very small commitment, the equivalent of wearing a campaign button. What would show a small investment in your activities? Can you engage someone to make a twenty-minute call, attend an in-person meeting, give you a room to host an event, make an important introduction?

Then think through the remaining steps (the equivalent of the bumper sticker, lawn sign, and so on) that you would like someone to take to be fully engaged with your activities. The more you can preplan those engagement steps, the better—after all, you don't want to start off by asking for the equivalent of a billboard on their roof. Of course, the counterargument is also at play here: don't hesitate to ask for a commitment of ideas, time, or even money. You are looking not only for interest in but also for engagement with your activities. If you meet with someone and they are open to partnership discussions, it won't do to simply leave a campaign button behind as you walk out. *How will you move people from your equivalent of a campaign button to a billboard with your name in lights on top of their (or their organization's) roof?*

Pick Your Engagement Strategies

At the start of your "campaign" to win over others (woo) to your *What If?* future, begin with individual and small-group meetings with potential sponsors, champions, and allies who already know and trust you. You are more likely to gain buy-in from those who already have a "reason to believe." These meetings will also help you hone your thinking as you learn what people align with and where you face significant pushback. If your network is small, don't use that as a reason to skip this step. Look for other opportunities to gain initial feedback:

Write a White Paper   In 2007, when Mary Hughes began to develop her ideas for how to improve the political landscape for women candidates, she crafted a white paper—a document that outlined her thesis, research, and potential strategies. She revised this document over the following two years, further ideating and researching, formulating and rethinking. As she sent this white paper out to potential allies and partners, she quickly identified those who were willing to align with her efforts and those who were not.

Create an Industry Consortium   After her initial success with the first PowerPathway programs, Van Ton-Quinlivan believed she had a model that was equally applicable to other utility companies. She convened an "industry consortium," identifying people who shared her job title or job responsibilities at the other major California utility companies and inviting them to join. At their quarterly meetings, consortium members discussed how to partner to create future PowerPathway programs, as well as how the other industry players could replicate the PowerPathway program in their own companies. In this way, she not only began to see her ideas adopted and replicated but also gained needed buy-in for larger efforts to extend the reach of the PowerPathway initiative.

Present a Training Event   Even before Steve Craft had completed the first TEDxNASA event, he began to think through what it would take to seed similar initiatives across other NASA centers. He had initially been turned down (and often stonewalled) by some of those he expected to be enthusiastic proponents. However, he did have one highly placed executive who was with him "110 percent" from the beginning. He made sure to give this champion credit, with prominent placement on the stage at the initial event. He did regular check-ins with her to ensure that he maintained her wholehearted participation throughout. To get to the next level, though, he knew he needed a team of folks from multiple locations willing to host a TEDxNASA event at their sites.

Craft created and hosted a training session designed to teach how to bring together a TEDx event. What did it take to get permission, find a site, identify the right speakers, engage the public, and so on? None of these were traditional skill sets for most NASA employees. Craft recognized that to get potential supporters on board, they needed firsthand experience of the event and a ready-made how-to kit to show them what to do every step of the way.[6]

Encourage a Spin-Off   In 1999, when I had been CEO of FWE full-time for about a year, I got a call from one of our members who had recently relocated to Seattle. She was interested in starting a chapter of our organization in the Pacific Northwest. I was immediately enthusiastic about the idea—I knew that the problems women faced in starting venture-funded businesses were far more challenging outside the Bay Area. I believed that there were several other cities where our proven programs could do a lot of good.

After much discussion over the next few months, the FWE board agreed to launch its first foray into replication. In the next three years, we expanded to Los Angeles, Orange County (California), Texas, Colorado, and even Paris, France. In each case, the success of our Bay Area initiatives and the press we received brought potential chapter leaders to our door, eager to create similar programs in their respective cities. The enthusiastic involvement of our friends, fans, and eventually our followers broadened our impact far beyond our initial endeavors, and together we helped thousands of women entrepreneurs build successful businesses.

Prepare Your Champions

In addition to testing your ideas with potential champions, it is also critical to empower them to step up and stand with you when necessary. I learned this the hard way when I first approached women in the venture community with the idea of hosting Springboard, the first venture conference for women. Rather than the enthusiasm I expected, I ran into a large contingent of naysayers and nervous Nellies. What if the event wasn't a big success? Would they be embarrassed in front of their male colleagues? Was an event like this really needed, they wondered?

Fortunately, I had a few key champions, including venture capitalists like Heidi Roizen and Helen Ingerson, whose actions on my behalf went far to overcome those objections. I learned the value of not only being prepared myself but also ensuring that my champions were fully invested, inspired, and informed so that they could act effectively on my behalf.

To identify and prepare a champion, follow this guide:

Find a member of the inner circle: If you are trying to win over a group of people, find someone from within that community. Someone who is well known, well respected, and well connected would be best, of course.

Make sure they are a believer: There is nothing worse than a halfhearted endorsement. Is your champion fully on board with what you are doing? You've heard the expression "damning with faint praise"? That applies here. If someone doesn't heartily and authentically engage, they're not right for this role.

Prepare talking points: Provide champions with some clear messages—even if you have to write their speech or talking points with them. Their message should be your message, not something they dreamed up. However, do rely on them to know what language will best resonate.

Develop engagement activities: Work with them to clearly spell out which engagement strategy is the best fit. They will also know best what to ask for—a check, volunteer time, and so on.

The last two of these strategies are the same ones you'd use if you were the one speaking about what you're doing. The difference is that your champions are more likely to be heard and believed and far more likely to elicit a positive response. Their credibility within the group you are trying to win over will get others on board.

In the next chapter, we are going to explore what else, besides preparing your champions, you can do to stay on track when you face objections or uncertainty about your next steps.

ACTIVATE YOUR ADVOCATES: A QUICK REVIEW

In this step of the thought leadership journey, successful thought leaders

- Recognize it's time to broaden their impact from one ripple to an entire pond
- Identify champions and allies whom they can align with to move their efforts forward substantially
- Think about "what's in it for them" and what holds people back, and align their messages accordingly
- Set up their tracking and connection tools, prepare their message template and one-page action plan, and rehearse and hone their elevator speech and key messages
- Pursue a "Button to Billboard" engagement strategy—incrementally bringing people on board
- Create broader agreement with their ideas—crafting a white paper, hosting a training, or encouraging a spin-off
- Identify and empower champions from key constituent communities

MORE FOOD FOR THOUGHT
Message Template

If you are unclear about what goes into your message template, I've provided a completed one below that will give you some ideas on how to move forward. No matter who you are or what you're doing, studying a completed message template will help you go far to hone your ideas, better "sell" your thinking, and win over others.

Example of a Completed Message Template

As closely as I can recall, this was our message when the Forum for Women Entrepreneurs cohosted the first Springboard Venture Conference in Silicon Valley in 2000.

> *Issue*: Women entrepreneurs receive less than 3 percent of the venture capital funding in the United States. This is primarily due to their lack of access to fundraising information, role models, and resource providers, as well as connections to funding sources. The Springboard Venture Conference will be the first venture conference exclusively for women entrepreneurs. It will provide a select group of twenty-five women running life science and technology companies with three months of coaching on their businesses, and then provide them access to the top angel and venture investors in the United States.

> *Summary*: Springboard is the first venture conference for women entrepreneurs and will provide all of the resources needed to overcome women's barriers to raising venture capital for their businesses.

> *Objective*: The mission of the Forum for Women Entrepreneurs (FWE) is to increase the success of

women who start and lead venture-fundable businesses. The Springboard event will be cohosted by FWE and the National Women's Business Council and will raise awareness of our organization and the issues we care about, and improve the statistics of women raising venture funding.

Audience/Constituents: investors, bankers, lawyers, accountants, and others who are part of the ecosystem of entrepreneurial businesses, as well as women entrepreneurs who might apply to participate in the program

Influencers: [a list of all of our sponsors, advisory committee, and funders—all big brand names that everyone had heard of]

What's in it for them: Investors will find companies to invest in. Bankers, lawyers, and accountants will find potential clients. Women entrepreneurs will find the resources and training they need to be successful, as well as media attention for their businesses. All of the participants will be a part of changing the road map for women entrepreneurs.

What holds them back: Women have not traditionally sought or received venture capital; it is hard to break into the "old boys' network" of venture capital; "this has never been done before" thinking.

Channels: news media, speeches, email, and smaller events, as well as partners and sponsors' channels of communication

Unspoken message: No one believes women entrepreneurs are building, or are capable of building, venture-fundable businesses, and we are going to prove them wrong.

(continued)

Spoken message: Sponsored by [a list of top sponsors], FWE, and the National Women's Business Council, Springboard is the first venture conference for women entrepreneurs.

Proof points: Data and statistics about the growth and potential of women entrepreneurs

FAQ: Here I would include the answers to questions like, Why should I support Springboard? Has a program like this been done before? Why aren't you doing a co-ed event? How did you select the women who are presenting? What investors are involved? What sponsors are involved? How much does it cost?

Keywords: Springboard Venture Conference, women entrepreneurs, venture capital, Forum for Women Entrepreneurs, National Women's Business Council, startups, fundraising, funding, start-up, small business, angel investors

CHAPTER 4

PUT YOUR "I" ON THE LINE

In the previous chapters, we discussed the first steps you will take to advance from leader to thought leader—how to identify your niche and your *What If?* future and begin to make the first ripples in your pond. But this transition is not exclusively about catalyzing conversations, building new initiatives, and securing buy-in from champions and allies. It is also an internal dialogue, one that often requires some soul-searching and the willingness to, as I call it, "put your 'I' on the line"—step into the spotlight as the person who is ready to lead the way.

"IF NOT ME, THEN WHO?"

One person who explains this transition well is Kathleen Harren, MSN MHA RN, of the Providence Little Company of Mary Medical Center in Torrance, California. During her career, Harren has progressed from director of nursing, to chief nurse executive, to regional director of the center's brand-new Nursing Institute. She has regularly been asked to speak across the country as a thought leader about California's nursing challenges. Harren admits that she first had to overcome her own concerns.

"I have always stepped forward, pretty often feeling not expert enough, and wondering or worrying whether or not I have the expertise to be a thought leader or contribute to a particular discussion with depth. I have second-guessed myself, doubting whether or not I was confident enough. But at the end of the day, I've realized that my experiences, in fact, have rendered me ready. And I think to myself, *if not me, then who?*"

For every leader and thought leader that's an important question. If not you, then who? When you discover the big problems that await you, when you watch the evening news, or when you observe first-hand the challenges ahead in your community or industry, you'll realize there is much work to be done. Sometimes this can be paralyzing. Yet Harren's advice, which I second wholeheartedly, is, "Don't hold yourself back; don't think that there's someone else out there." This chapter is about how to take the next step forward, even when you are too tired or confused or you don't know the way.

Whenever I speak about this aspect of thought leadership, I use an image that to me sums it up beautifully. It is a picture of a tiny orange kitten seated before a beautiful antique mirror. In the mirror he sees reflected back at him not his own tiny kitten self but instead an enormous orange lion, calm and majestic.

People connect with this image for many reasons. Whether we like to admit it or not, we've all been that kitten looking in the mirror. Depending on what messages we tell ourselves, whom we surround ourselves with, or how things are going in our lives, we see ourselves reflected as a lion with more or less frequency.

What helps us stay connected to our inner lion? What do we need to have in place in order to step forward and take our place at the table—to put our "I" on the line? I believe this involves facing our responsibilities to our own gifts, as well as to our communities and organizations and our world, what I call "finding your imperative." And over and over along the way this requires facing your fears, fostering your resilience, and asking for help.

FIND YOUR IMPERATIVE

What if thought leadership is not a "maybe, someday" proposition? What if instead it's an obligation? What if, when you look ahead to the day when you will be the recognized go-to person, you were filled not with doubt but with a sense of responsibility—an imperative—to do your part?

Katie Orenstein is the founder and CEO of the OpEd Project. Her organization encourages budding thought leaders to think about their expertise and then trains them how to write effective opinion pieces and get them published in the major media. She argues, "By not sharing our stories and not telling our version of the world, then someone else is telling our world for us. If we are not giving all of our best ideas to the world, then the best ideas and the best minds are missing—at a collective cost to society. Many of us are walking through life as if our knowledge and our experience doesn't matter, but what if it did?"[1]

The truth is, none of us got here on our own. We all have a responsibility to serve as the inspiration and the role model for those who follow behind us. As change agents with important efforts under way, I believe it is our responsibility and even our obligation to take the stage and push our ideas forward.

One of the people who faced that responsibility—who found she needed to take her place at the head of a movement—was Commander Zoe Dunning, SC, USNR (Ret.).

CASE STUDY: ZOE DUNNING

When Commander Zoe Dunning joined the U.S. Navy, she was seventeen years old. Her class at the United States Naval Academy in Annapolis was one of the first to include women. She selected the Naval Academy because it stood for honor, integrity, and service and she felt their honor code was consistent with her own. When she entered the academy, she told me she would have "identified myself as asexual," but once she was there, she came to realize she was a lesbian. She also quickly grasped that she needed to hide that fact, as she watched other suspected lesbian midshipmen investigated and discharged.

Dunning found herself in a situation where she "had to lie in order to maintain a relationship with the organization" she had joined. But she "so badly wanted to serve [her] country, [she] was willing to pay the price" by keeping her personal life a secret. After graduating from the academy, she stayed in the military for six years and then applied and was accepted to Stanford Business School. While there, she maintained her reserve status because "I felt I had something to contribute," and the small sum she earned in the reserves helped to pay her tuition.

Around this time, Bill Clinton was elected president, and one of his campaign promises was to lift the ban on gays serving in the military. Dunning was "very excited about that; having seen the damage and destruction the policy had done to friends and colleagues, I thought that was the right thing to do." Unfortunately, Clinton immediately came under pressure to retract his commitment; rallies were quickly organized across the United States to bring publicity to his campaign promise.

When Dunning was given an opportunity to speak at one of these rallies, "The speech just started composing itself in my head," she told me. "I wanted to talk about what my experience was like, and what the experiences of others around me were, and why the policy was wrong.

"The thing that was so frustrating to me was if you look at any current issue—whether healthcare reform, financial reform— those who are impacted by the decisions have the chance to speak up for themselves. They can lobby Congress, they can talk to the media, they can tell their story. But in this case, the folks who were impacted, the gays and lesbians in the military, could not speak on their own behalf. They were forced to be silent in this debate. So, you had politicians talking, you had the media talking, you had gay rights activists talking, but you didn't actually have people whose lives were on the line participating in the conversation."

At the time she was invited to speak, Dunning was in her final year of business school and already had a job lined up with Deloitte Consulting. She had a stellar military record and she was a graduate of one of the most prestigious institutions in the military. She knew she risked being discharged if she spoke out, but she also felt it was important to be, as her mother had always told her, "part of the solution."

She could "sit on the sidelines and complain of the injustice," or she could speak out. With her record, she might be heard. Dunning "very much believes that leadership is by example—you put yourself on the line and do as you ask others to do." At the end of the day, she felt it was her "duty to give voice to those who were impacted by the policy, those who could not speak up."

After she spoke at the rally, a small article about the event appeared in the newspaper, and no surprise to anyone, the following weekend the military started discharge procedures. Dunning was one of the first military members to be prosecuted under the "Don't Ask, Don't Tell" law, and her case dragged on for more than two years. Her pro bono attorneys spent almost a half million dollars representing her. In the end, however, she prevailed. In fact, she was the only individual to ever win a case under the law. Dunning continued to serve as the only openly gay member of the U.S. military for the next thirteen years, even receiving a promotion to lieutenant commander and then commander.

Dunning spoke to me about the toll on her personally, the reactions of her colleagues—who felt she was embarrassing the military or making them look bad by her actions—and what it took to keep going. As she described it, "You feel the pressure to represent your entire community; you are one person representing all of these people; you want to do well by it."

In addition to serving as a role model, Dunning began speaking publicly, doing numerous press interviews and actively lobbying Congress to repeal "Don't Ask, Don't Tell." She found that many people had assumptions and stereotypes about what it was like to serve under the policy, and she did her best to let them know the real truth. When she did, "they sort of came on board."

She also helped found a nonprofit, the Servicemembers Legal Defense Network (SLDN), which provided a legal advice hotline and other resources to service members who might face retaliation for even the suspicion of being gay in the military. Finally, eighteen years after she began her battle for equality in the Armed Forces, President Barack Obama honored her by inviting her to stand next to him when he signed the historic Don't Ask, Don't Tell Repeal Act of 2010.[2]

Whether or not you agree with her actions, when Commander Dunning stepped into the limelight and became the face of her community (and the target of many people both inside and outside the military hierarchy), for her it was not optional. It was an imperative. Standing for her community was not an act of whimsy; it was an act of courage. Her eighteen-year battle was not for herself, for her ego, for self-aggrandizement, or for glory. It was the right thing to do—because she could and so many others couldn't.

As you face your own roadblocks, stop and remind yourself why you are on this journey. In what way are you committed to making a contribution? What agenda will you move forward for yourself or a larger constituency? Will your having a seat at the table give a boost to others who have no chance of achieving that seat themselves? Are you the spokesperson for those who may never have an opportunity for their voice to be heard? What difference can you make to advance the agenda of the people you represent?

When you find the way forward blocked or find that your ideas are initially rejected, I invite you to revisit your *What If?* future. Ask yourself if anyone else sees that future as clearly as you do or has as much commitment to making that future possible. If not, then perhaps it is imperative, as it was for Commander Dunning, for you to be part of the solution, even if it takes time, energy, dedication; even if it's at the risk of your reputation, your friendships, or your career. Sometimes being willing to take a risk, to see yourself as "the one," makes it possible to bring about transformative change—though it may take eighteen years.

Followers Can Lead, Too

I need to take a small detour here. Some people may read the section above and think, *There is actually someone else. I am not the only one. Someone else does see the future as clearly as I do (or maybe more clearly) and has as much commitment as I do to make that future possible.* Maybe you think, *I don't really need to step up here. They are carrying the flag, and I can stay in the background, quietly doing my part without having any spotlight on me.*

Perhaps you work for a well-known CEO or a well-respected executive director. Or maybe someone else came up with the ideas that you are proselytizing or started the venture that you now lead. Perhaps you're thinking, *They've got this*, or, *I don't want to steal their thunder*, or even, *Nothing I have to say is really very original.*

But I would look at it differently. Followers are actually leaders in disguise. Without followers, nothing much happens. One of the people who weighed in on this very effectively is Derek Sivers. If you haven't seen his talk "How to Start a Movement" on YouTube, it's worth a watch.[3] His premise is that it is often not the leader whom others are following when they join a movement; it is the "first follower," the first person to get on board with an idea. Once the "first follower" is on board, it is safe for others to participate. The barriers are lowered for the next person to join.

When you visibly assume the role of first follower, you will make any change you're espousing or any movement you care to bring about that much more likely to succeed. But perhaps you're worried about something else entirely?

A Word About Self-Promotion

Guy Kawasaki, best-selling author of *APE: Author, Publisher, Entrepreneur—How to Publish a Book*, is frequently called on to talk with individuals who are considering writing their first book.[4] During one of those conversations, he received an interesting question from his audience, one that I often hear at my talks: "Is all this [writing a book, speaking, and so on] just self-promotion?"

Kawasaki said he is always surprised by this question. He turned back to the audience and asked, "Is what you're doing of value? If so, then keep going. It is not self-promoting if you are adding value to the world."[5]

I couldn't agree more. Rather than being concerned about whether others will interpret your actions as bragging, recognize the value of sharing new ideas and new ways of thinking; envision yourself as the spokesperson or the evangelist for the innovation or improvement you want to see in the world.

Nancy Calderon is a global lead partner at KPMG, one of the largest professional services firms in the world. Throughout her career, she has developed a reputation as a champion for women. In addition to her client and organizational responsibilities, Calderon chairs KPMG's Women's Advisory Board, addressing issues and initiatives supporting women's professional development and advancement in the workplace. She is also a member of KPMG's Diversity Advisory Board. When she first stepped into the spotlight as a spokesperson on behalf of women's issues, she did so because it was the right thing to do. Now, as one of the senior-most women executives in the accounting industry, Calderon's visible presence in the broader women's community has helped her organization attract and retain high-performing women leaders.[6]

Take the Long View

Creating a movement doesn't happen overnight. Peter Schwartz, the futurist and longtime evangelist of scenario planning, told me, "When I was very young, I was given a piece of advice and it was very influential. A very dear friend said to me, 'If it doesn't take fifty years, it isn't worth doing, and if you really want to make a big impact, it usually takes a while.'"[7] How true!

Whenever I get discouraged about the lack of progress in my own endeavors, I try to think about Dr. Maulana Karenga, who has been working for the rights of African Americans, and Gloria Steinem, who has been working for the rights of women, each for more than forty years. As founders of their movements, they have welcomed any number of followers along the way—many of whom developed thought leadership platforms of their own. Still others will be needed to pick up their torch and carry it, long after they're gone.

I am not saying that every change takes fifty years. Thank goodness! But no matter how you envision your *What If?* future—whether you are fighting to reverse an injustice or hoping to encourage people to think in new ways; whether you have begun to alter the direction of a Fortune 500 company or have not yet launched your first program, project, or organization—remember that being a change agent requires that you take the long view. Find others to help. Even from the beginning, think about who can carry the torch after you're gone. (We'll talk more about this in Chapter Seven.)

OVERCOME YOUR FEARS

Thought leaders face a lot of different fears along the way: fear of failure, fear of being judged, fear of being vulnerable, fear of letting others down, even fear of success. Many don't step into the spotlight because they are not yet "expert" enough, even when they know far more than everyone around them. Others fear that everything they have to say has already been said, even when they have a unique point of view that others need to hear. And some hold themselves back because they are too young or too old or don't have the right job, the right title, or the right degree.

For me, it's often a fear of the judgment of my peers—is what I have to say "good enough" or "smart enough" to measure up?

Will others read what I write or hear what I have to say and think, *She's not that original* or *She has nothing new to say?* You may be thinking, *But you wrote a whole book*—you *obviously have something to say*. True, but that doesn't mean I didn't get stuck, sometimes for weeks, along the way. Our fears are our fears. You'll have yours, I have mine. They may not be rational or justified, but they can still be paralyzing.

When I get stopped by my fears—rational or not—I try to shift the prism a little bit to find a new perspective. I look around me and find people who have done what I want to do or those who are doing big things regardless of their fears. You notice I didn't say find people without fears. We all have fears. Some (like Hank Leber, Melissa Anderson, Nikki Gilmore, and Robin Chase—see below) have learned to reframe them in new ways.

It's All Just Learning   The young entrepreneur Hank Leber, cofounder and CEO of GonnaBe, believes, "Failure doesn't even really exist. If something doesn't go the way that you planned it to go, and you learn from it, that's just called learning. That's not really failure. Failure is if you keep doing the same wrong things over and over; you're not really making progress. Otherwise, it's just learning—and learning is good! So, if your goal is to learn as much as possible as you go, instead of your goal is to not fail, then you can keep on going and going and going."[8] *What do you still need to learn?*

Trust the Risk/Respect Feedback Loop   In a 2010 article, Melissa J. Anderson and Nikki Gilmore had another unique viewpoint. They wrote, "When you take a big risk to put your big idea into motion, your energy and passion and commitment to your idea convinces the people who respect you to come on board, and take that risk with you. When that big risk delivers, they'll respect you more as a leader. As their respect for you grows, so does your confidence and ability to undertake risky endeavors. It's a big *risk–respect feedback loop*."[9] *What big risk can you take to earn more respect?*

Be a Role Model   A well-known transportation innovator, Robin Chase was honored by *Time* magazine as among the "100 Most Influential People in the World" in 2009. I asked her why she agrees to leave her home in Boston and her business (she is the CEO of her third start-up, Buzzcar, a car-sharing marketplace) to accept over fifty (mostly unpaid) speaking engagements a year. She told me she was inspired by a talk she heard by the late Ann Richards, the former governor of Texas, about the importance of role models.

"She made us laugh and cry. She inspired us," Chase recalls about her experience seeing Ann Richards speak. "One of the many things she said—and I still remember it, although it was more than ten years ago—'As women leaders, you should never turn down a speaking engagement. There are too few women doing amazing things. So you have to be up there as a role model.'"[10] I would say there are far too few *people* doing amazing things, and I'd encourage everyone reading this book to see themselves as a role model. *For whom are you a role model? What can you do to inspire others?*

FOSTER YOUR RESILIENCE

Whether you are getting started, or are well on your way, the truth is you will run into bumps in the road: people who are reluctant to participate in your *What If?* future, those who will stand in your way, and even a few that might actively work to sabotage your success. It is, sadly, almost always so for those pushing for transformation in the world.

A few years ago, two former business school professors of mine, Professor Jeffrey Pfeffer, author of *Power*, and Jim Collins, author of *Good to Great*, did an informal study of my Stanford MBA classmates to discern what factors were the most influential in determining which students would "make it" and which would not. (As I recall, they were not looking for those who had made it as measured by dollars earned, but those who were most successful all around in achieving their goals and dreams.) After eliminating many different factors, they landed on *resilience* as the one defining skill and behavior that allowed some to stand out from the rest. After all, it wasn't that none of us faced adversity—we all did. But some were able to pick themselves up and brush themselves off and move on, while others were not.

Resilience counts.

As I wrote this book, I kept looking for some basic "rules for resilience" that you could take forward through your own thought leadership journey. What can you do to stay on track, get back on track, and stay motivated when things don't go your way? Here are a few rules that I've compiled.

Avoid the Black and White   The nurse leader, Kathleen Harren, has met with "a fair amount of criticism" in her career. But when she has chosen to "stand out there and be clear about how I see the world," she has found one way to do this that has led to fewer arrows and more dialogue. She has learned to say, "This is how I see it. This is my worldview." She believes it is important to avoid black-and-white or absolutist statements, and instead "to state things as my opinion, based on my experience." *How can you best frame your ideas so that they remain strong and clear while allowing others with different views to hear and understand?*

Get Comfortable Not Knowing   To Harren, the biggest learning for every individual "is the need to get comfortable and to [be able to] speak on any particular issue without being fully prepared. To be flexible and articulate and confident enough," even when you don't know everything, because "we can't know everything." To gain that confidence for herself, she has taken several courses on how to be an effective storyteller as well as media training in order to improve her skills and confidence in front of the microphone. *What can you do to get prepared for when you're not prepared?*

Practice Just-in-Time Learning   Harren believes that "it's almost impossible to be an expert today." She regularly finds that she is doing a lot of "just-in-time informing on particular issues." However, she has also learned that "reading and being informed on the issues of the day has really been essential—you can't be a storyteller without having facts."[11] Stay generally well informed and go deep on an issue when you need to. *What can you do to stay generally informed in your niche? How can you anticipate the big questions your organization or industry will face?*

Fire the Itty-Bitty-Shitty Committee   One of my clients, Antonia Galindo, talks about the importance of firing your "itty-bitty-shitty committee"—those voices in your head that essentially tell you that you are never going to be successful, so why start anyway?[12] Sometimes this requires having a cheerleader (or a team of them) to remind you how wonderful you are and that you should keep going. Others find different approaches. Chip Conley, founder and former CEO of Joie de Vivre Hospitality, wrote four successful books while he was a full-time CEO. He found that the best strategy for avoiding his negative voices was to wake up to write at 3:30 or 4:00 in the morning, because then "his brain was awake, but his critic wasn't."[13] *How can you fire or quiet your inner critic? Who can serve as your cheerleader?*

Use "Up Until Now"   We all have excuses that we've used for years that keep us from moving forward. "I'm not good at asking for help," "I don't have time," "I'm not good at delegating" are some of the common ones I hear from clients. Author and life-balance expert Mary LoVerde suggests you add the phrase "up until now" in front of those excuses, and take the time to identify new behaviors that can serve you—starting today.[14] Thought leadership requires that you take a leap of faith and make a personal commitment to put yourself first. The more you do, the easier it gets. *What habits or excuses have you used "up until now" that it's time to leave by the wayside?*

Celebrate the Small Wins   When Van Ton-Quinlivan first launched the PowerPathway initiative at Pacific Gas and Electric, a one-hundred-year-old utility company, she realized that change was not going to happen overnight. Every time she had one small win—a new stakeholder got on board with her ideas; she received authorization to hire one staff person; her team got some press attention—she wrote that "win" on a yellow sticky note and hung it on the wall outside her office. Every morning as she came down the hall, those notes served as her reminders that she was indeed making progress.

Create Refreshment Practices   Mary LoVerde and Kathy Harren both advocate building in some refreshment practices to your day. They both have a meditation practice; Kathy reads the "provocative poets" like Maya Angelou and David Whyte; and Mary has a series of affirmations she reads twice a day. They both are big promoters of staying active. Kathy recommends you "get out and walk and see the world in new ways."[15] Mary is an avid amateur ballroom dancer, something she took up in her fifties. *What refreshment practices could you introduce into your life that could help you stay on track?*

Focus on the Next Twenty-Four Hours   Leah Busque is the founder and CEO of TaskRabbit, Inc., an online marketplace for people looking for others to do simple tasks. She and her husband came up with the idea for the company in 2008. Although she had never run a start-up, four months later she quit her job at IBM and by 2012 they were live in nine cities. Her advice to others with similar ambitions is to get up every day and ask yourself, "How can I push this business forward in the next twenty-four hours?"[16] *What could you do each day to push forward the change you want to see in the world?*

See Yourself as a Force Multiplier for Good   When Ali Wing founded her company, giggle.com, a now highly successful online baby products store, she never expected she would be the personality of the giggle brand. "I am an operational CEO, not just a spokesperson for the brand. Being out speaking and doing TV is time-consuming. But the more media I do, the more I connect to the folks who are our customers." What keeps her going when she's tired or not all that excited about getting dressed up to go on TV again? "I ask myself, 'Am I a force multiplier for good—someone who is multiplying the good in the world?' and if the answer is yes, then I keep going. I don't overanalyze; I stay in motion, defining and refining our message and telling our story in an engaging way."[17] *How can you become a force multiplier for good?*

Ask, Am I Playing a Big Game?   Entrepreneur Todd Beauchamp, president of a very innovative home theater company called In2Technologies, keeps himself going with two simple questions: "Am I playing a big game?" and "Is this concern I have today something worth taking me out of that game?" Given that he is re-inventing the home theater market almost singlehandedly, Beauchamp knows he's playing a very big game, and he has yet to find any obstacles that are worth giving up his dream.[18] *Are you playing a big game? Are your concerns worthy of taking you out of that game?*

See Feedback as a Gift   Joanna Bloor, vice president at Pandora, has learned to look at feedback as a gift. She reminds herself of the words of Diane Sawyer: "Criticism is just a really bad way of making a request." Thus, when she gets negative feedback, she looks at it as a request to "be even more awesome."[19] *When you get feedback, what is the request that is really hidden within?*

Embrace Failure   Some organizations publish "failure reports" every year alongside their annual reports. "I only let the best failures into the report," Ashley Good, former "Head of Failure" at Engineers Without Borders Canada and author of their annual failure report, told the *New York Times*.[20] "The examples that are published," she said, show people who are "taking risks to be innovative." The world would be a very different place if we were all taking more risks—or encouraged to do so. That reminds me of a sign I once saw on the exit door of the office of a local start-up that read, "Let's Make Better Mistakes Tomorrow." That's embracing failure! *Could you create a failure report at the end of each year to celebrate your failures and your willingness to take risks? What sign do you need to put on your wall to encourage you to keep taking big risks?*

Remind Yourself Why   I am always looking for great life strategies, and I find them in the most unexpected places. One that I adopted a few years ago is so simple that I'm still surprised it works. Think about the top ten reasons why you want to be a thought leader. Write them on a 3x5 index card and prop the card next to your bed (or type it into your phone). Read the card first thing in the morning and last thing at night.[21] This will keep you focused on the *why*, which is often the single biggest motivator for any of us to achieve anything. (This exercise can be helpful for any effort you have under way.) *What* why *do you want to write on your index card?*

FIND (LOTS OF) HELP

Speaking of "why," why is it that after we have gained experience or credentials in one arena we tend to believe that we should be able to figure everything out all by ourselves, no matter how far outside our comfort zone. In most cases our "go it alone" instincts are exactly wrong. Instead what we need is to find help, in whatever way it can be arranged. In fact, the very best rule for resilience I know is to line up lots of different kinds of help as often as possible.

Create a Brain Trust or Mastermind Group

One thing that has made me happier, calmer, and more successful over the last three years has been my "mastermind group." The concept of the mastermind group was formally introduced by Napoleon Hill in the early 1900s. In his classic book about success, *Think and Grow Rich*, he wrote about the mastermind principle as "The coordination of knowledge and effort of two or more people, who work toward a definite purpose, in the spirit of harmony." He continued, "No two minds ever come together without thereby creating a third, invisible intangible force, which may be likened to a third mind."[22] This third mind, or mastermind, allows every participant to be more successful.

There are many organized groups (mastermind groups, essentially) for entrepreneurs, including Vistage, Entrepreneur's Organization, Young Presidents Organization, and Women Presidents Organization. Those I know who have participated in these groups swear by them. If you're not an entrepreneur, you can still find a mastermind group: search for communities of practice, academies, or Meetup groups in your niche.

You can also form your own. Identify two to eleven individuals who share a common goal with you, say to develop a thought leadership platform, grow a business, write a book, or become a better speaker. Make sure there are no direct competitors in the group. Develop some ground rules about how often to meet and how the meetings will be facilitated. (My group meets whenever we are in the same area, or when we can manufacture excuses to be in the same area, as we all live in different cities. We also talk on the phone about once a month, and we email frequently.) Don't let one person dominate the group, and of course confidentiality is key. The most critical requirement is a commitment to "have each other's backs *and* each other's fronts."

There is no limit on what can be discussed. Share best practices, get feedback on your ideas, or discuss challenging issues or setbacks. Test a new speech or story before delivering it to a larger audience.

Celebrate one another's successes, and stand behind each other when things go awry. For me, this has become the safe place to share what isn't working or to seek advice when I have no idea what to do next. The two women in my mastermind group are both much more experienced speakers and authors and they show me the path forward; I have a lot of editing, technical, and social media skills that I can offer to them. *Who belongs on your mastermind team?*

Create a Purse Club

A few years ago, I attended a dinner and lecture event at a local university. Just before the presentation began, a woman entered the room and hurriedly took the last seat at our table. Surprisingly, as she sat down, she placed her purse right in front of her, on the table. Despite the dinnerware, wineglasses, and butter plates, and the waiters scurrying to and fro, she left it there throughout the meal.

After the program was over, I made a point of saying to her, "What a beautiful purse—where did you get it?" She broke out in a huge smile and told me, "I got it from my purse club!"

I was instantly intrigued.

She explained, "A few years ago my friend and I realized that no one was coming to help us with our careers. We decided to form our own purse club. Each of us committed to help the other in whatever ways we could—I might invite her to attend a business networking event with me and introduce her to someone she needs to meet; she might send me a job listing for a job that is a great fit for me. When one of us is preparing for an interview, the other will spend hours brainstorming questions and critiquing answers. And when something works out that was due to our friend's help, to say thank you we give each other a purse.

"When we first started the club, neither of us had any money, so the purses were really tiny. But things are a little different now." She smiled again, and held up her very beautiful purse. "My friend just got a great new job, and I just got this really great purse." *Who will you invite to join your purse club? Or maybe you'd prefer a fishing rod club? (Personally, I always prefer chocolate.)*

Build Your Own Personal Board of Directors

Long before I knew about purse clubs and mastermind teams, a mentor of mine recommended I build my own personal board of directors. This type of trusted advisory group works well for start-ups and Fortune 500 CEOs, she advised, so why can't you have one of your very own?

Great idea!

My personal board's members don't really know they are part of a team—they likely each think they are the only one I call when I need a sounding board. I have never convened them as a group or introduced one of them to the others. But together they have provided excellent advice on career and life decisions or have been a shoulder to cry on. Of course you can hire a coach (and for long-term issues, I highly recommend it), but for the day-to-day decisions and challenges that we all face, a personal board of directors is more efficient.

My board includes the husband of a friend of mine, who is exceptionally good at negotiating anything; it includes an old boss who shares my career interests and pushes me outside my comfort zone, a former colleague who is extremely well connected, and others whom I have "picked up" along the way. I do not call each of them for every decision, but I perhaps most regret those times when I did not make a call that I should have.

As with a real board, you'll receive contradictory advice from the members of your personal board of directors. When I decided to switch careers and join a political campaign for a year, my board members did not unanimously acclaim this as the right direction. (Looking back, I wish I'd paid more attention to those who tried to dissuade me!) It will always be up to you whether you take the advice you receive. Just don't hesitate to ask for it. *Who belongs on your personal board of directors?*

LET GO OF YOUR "YEAH, BUT"

In the middle of writing this book, I met an amazing woman who had recently been honored as one of the top one hundred attorneys in Silicon Valley. I was urging her to get out and speak about her expertise, not solely as an instructor in a legal setting but more broadly at industry conferences, where she could share her expertise in negotiation tactics and creating win-win mergers.

Her response? "Yeah, but . . ." and then she stopped.

"Yeah, but what?" I asked.

It turns out that although she had been recognized by her peers for her achievements in a highly competitive marketplace, and had twenty-plus years working in her field, she was still worried that if she put herself forward as an expert, someone might say, "What do you know about negotiations?"

Wow. I guess even after you've "arrived" you can still worry that others might not think so. We all have our "Yeah, but . . ."

Yours might be related to being too old or too young, too tall or too short, too fat or too skinny. You might come from a culture that encourages you not to step into the spotlight or from a family that tells you it's not polite to brag. You might think you don't know enough, or you may be worried that others won't like you if you stand out from the crowd or say something controversial. Or you may have watched other thought leaders get attacked or vilified for their ideas and worry the same might happen to you.

We all have our "Yeah, but . . ." Don't let yours take you out of the game. And know that I, for one, am cheering for you from the sidelines. Please keep going.

Now with your "I" solidly on the line, your internal critic at bay, and your external support system around you, you are ready for the next chapter: pulling together your knowledge and lessons learned and creating a blueprint for others to follow.

PUT YOUR "I" ON THE LINE:
A QUICK REVIEW

In this step of the thought leadership journey, successful thought leaders

- Are willing to step forward, even if they are not yet expert enough
- Understand that it is their right and responsibility to lend their voice to the world's conversations
- Have the courage to stand up for their community, even if there is personal risk
- Recognize that even as a follower they too have a role: to pick up the torch and carry it forward
- Look at failure as just a step in learning
- Appreciate the surprising rewards—influence, impact, connections—that come with stepping into the spotlight of thought leadership
- Use the "rules for resilience" to reframe any doubts or fears and overcome failures and setbacks
- Use different kinds of help: forming a mastermind group, "purse club," or personal board of directors to support their efforts
- Leave aside their "Yeah, but . . ." and keep moving forward

MORE FOOD FOR THOUGHT

Checklist for Overcoming Obstacles

Recapping the tools for reframing, resilience, and reflection given in this chapter, here are questions to ask yourself when you run into resistance (internal or external) on your journey:

✓ Is it time to give myself permission to move forward?

✓ Have I found an imperative for what I'm setting out to do?

✓ For whom do I serve as a role model?

✓ Am I playing a big game?

✓ Will I look back a year from now and think that what was holding me back today was worth stopping for?

✓ If I am one of many working on this idea or initiative, what is my role to play (for example, "first follower," leader, champion, sponsor, ally)?

✓ What steps can I take to make sure I am always learning?

✓ Can I be comfortable not knowing everything and learning more as I go along?

✓ What's one thing I can do to step into risk today?

✓ How can I celebrate the risks I'm taking, even if they result in failure?

✓ What can I do in the next twenty-four hours to move my ideas forward?

✓ Can I let go of old behaviors and fire the negative voices that hold me back?

✓ What can I do to refresh and renew so that I am motivated to move forward?

✓ Am I a "force multiplier for good"? In what ways?

✓ Who can help me? Should I form a mastermind group, "purse club," or personal board of directors?

✓ Can I reframe my "Yeah, but . . ." thinking to "Yes, I can!"?

CHAPTER 5

CODIFY YOUR LESSONS LEARNED

In earlier chapters, we spoke about how to find your niche or pond, start the first ripples in that pond, and then how to identify and align with allies and champions who can help you increase your impact. In the preceding chapter, we discussed the internal work you need to do to step into the spotlight and claim your role as a thought leader.

In this chapter, we are going to talk about how to codify your lessons learned, that is, formulate a methodology, framework, or set of guiding principles so that others may join with you to achieve your *What If?* future. When you create intellectual property—when you develop something that is uniquely yours, which you have exclusive rights to—you will further differentiate yourself as a thought leader, create greater momentum for your ideas, and potentially generate income to scale your impact more widely.

Some people have no trouble looking back as they complete a project, and they can easily tell you exactly what the key takeaways were. Or they can come up with a clever way to frame their ideas so that weeks later everyone is repeating what they said. Others love to distill complex ideas into a simple diagram, system, or approach that is easy to understand and replicate. Still others regularly create books, manuals, or even curricula so they can scale their ideas broadly.

Not so for me. This is the step I have struggled with the most.

I am a start-up person; I love to start things—nonprofits, conferences, companies. But it doesn't interest me all that much to figure out what I did and then explain it or systemize it, and that has been to my detriment over the years.

In fact, I can recall the day I decided to leave my corporate job at Motorola: it was the day I received the 300-page "Brand Guidelines Manual" from corporate headquarters; the whole document gave me the willies. I wanted to figure things out for myself, not have each step prescribed. That would hinder my creativity! Further, I am sure that I am the only successful product manager in the twenty-year history of Broderbund (the software company I worked for in the late 1980s and early 1990s) who actually prided herself on never having read the "Product Manager Handbook."

You get the picture. This is not my forte.

But that doesn't mean it's not important. In fact, what I've learned over the years is this: *Clarifying lessons learned and standardizing and systematizing a repeatable process into intellectual property is the step that most clearly separates the thought leaders whose ideas are sustained from those whose are not.*

Every year millions of thought leaders with amazing ideas successfully create bold initiatives, programs, and products, and many gain a successful following for those ideas. But to build momentum for new ways of thinking, to reframe an industry or pioneer sustained evolutionary or revolutionary change, you need to document what you know into a system, methodology, process, protocol, or set of guiding principles so others can easily understand, get on board, and help you replicate your ideas.

That's when real transformation is possible.

I think most of us change agents never take this step because we don't understand how new ideas are adopted. We are in the category of people who accept and readily adapt to new innovations and new ways of thinking—without a manual. But to create and propagate transformational change, not only do we need to lead people to think in new ways; we need to empower others to lead change in our absence. Thus, we must consider how changes get adopted, not just by those who embrace new ideas but also by those who are more prone to resist.

UNDERSTAND HOW CHANGE HAPPENS

Chip and Dan Heath, in their book *Switch: How to Change Things When Change Is Hard*, have a useful metaphor for the mechanism of change.[1] They talk about the "Rider"—our rational mind, which loves change—and the "Elephant"—our emotional mind, which loves comfort. They posit that the Elephant (given its propensity to resist anything that takes it out of its comfort zone) must be encouraged or redirected in order to allow the Rider (which has a much longer-term and more visionary view) to take charge.

This is accomplished when we focus on what the Heaths call "bright spots," initial efforts that are already showing promise and progress. These bright spots inspire hope that change is possible and let people see that things are on the right track. Then we (as change agents) need to help people overcome their "decision paralysis," that feeling we all get when there are so many possible directions to go that we can't make up our mind. The Heaths recommend that leaders provide this help by "scripting the critical moves"—spelling out the exact next steps needed to bring about change, thereby giving people a sense of a path forward. (Think of it as creating your own how-to kit or franchise manual.)

OVERCOME THE "NOT ME" ATTITUDE

How do you identify the bright spots you have already brought about and then script the critical moves so that others can follow your lead? What's required first is to overcome the "Not Me" attitude. The "Not Me" attitude varies for each of us who avoid the codifying and documenting step, but it often includes one or more of the following (often false) beliefs:

Not the leader: I was part of a team. I can't take credit for anything if I did not lead the initiative.

Others already know it or own it: There is nothing unique in what I did. Everyone knows it already, or the framework I used was created by others.

Too busy: I'm too busy making things happen to codify what I've learned.

My strengths lie elsewhere: I really don't enjoy documenting things; that's someone else's problem. (This is where I get stuck.)

Early days: We haven't made any progress yet—there aren't any bright spots.

Let me address each of these beliefs in turn.

Not the Leader   The Honorable Carol A. Beier, a justice of the Kansas Supreme Court, recalls something she learned in her first course on legal process: *the power of the first draft.*

Even though she risked being seen as taking a "woman's duties," she learned early in her career to relish the chance to take the minutes of a meeting or craft the first draft of an opinion. That way she got to put her stamp on the document first. She found that others rarely made significant modifications after the first draft was complete. They were content to let her set the direction if she was willing to do the heavy lifting of going first.[2]

You may not be seeking a seat on the Kansas Supreme Court, but the premise is the same. As the member of the team who writes down what happened, you have the opportunity to shape the story. You determine what gets highlighted and which path others will follow when they tread in your team's footsteps. You may not have led the initial initiative and you may not get your name up in lights, but you will play an important role in making progress possible and will prevent others from re-inventing the wheel. The better you do at crafting the blueprint, the more likely others will follow in your path. You'll also have the opportunity to name the guideposts along the way.

Others Already Know It or Own It   This attitude tends to be shaped by several assumptions. One of them is that whatever we've created can't be all that special; everyone must already know what we know, right? Wrong. The truth is that your unique perspective is just that: unique. Your background, experiences, the talents of other individuals you've worked with, and any challenging circumstances you've overcome all inform your perspective. Yes, you've built on the learning of others. Others will also build on what you've learned. But only if you've honored the fact that those experiences are worth sharing.

Another common assumption is that if you have been part of implementing an existing framework (for example, the Malcolm Baldrige quality standards, or the Magnet Recognition Program) or executing a set of existing tools or methodologies in your organization (web analytics, employee engagement surveys), then you cannot claim your own thought leadership in that arena. Yet, there is still much for others to learn from your experience. Your bright spots are the lessons you learned about how to simplify, streamline, or modernize an already standardized framework or process. Others want to hear your stories, inspiring or otherwise. Not only will you help them stay motivated; you'll help them avoid the same pitfalls along the way. (See the case study of Avinash Kaushik in Chapter Six for someone who did this very effectively.)

Too Busy   When I was at FWE, I always perceived myself as too busy to write things down. I'm sure you can relate. Yet, I've since learned that documenting a replicable set of steps should be built into the process of creating something new, whether you are undertaking an event, activity, initiative, or product. When you take the time to capture the lessons learned and add a "debrief step" to your planning process, you will begin to make headway here.

My Strengths Lie Elsewhere   Early in my career, I thought I lacked the expertise to create a unique methodology, or the capability to document my lessons learned in a way that others would find useful. If you feel the same way, my recommendation is to find others—early team members or participants in your activities—who will take on this responsibility. Alternatively, consult with (or hire) a professional—a curriculum developer or knowledge management expert. Are there individuals in your organization or industry who can offer you some advice?

Early Days   If you are just getting started, you're in luck. This chapter will outline exactly what you can do to get on the right track right from the beginning.

No matter what has been holding you back, I invite you to let go of any "Not Me" thinking and take the time to explore the ideas and exercises in this chapter. You'll learn how to capture your bright spots and script the critical moves for others as you document what you know and create intellectual property that is memorable, repeatable, measureable, verifiable, actionable, protectable, *and* uniquely yours.

CAPTURE WHAT YOU KNOW

As I interviewed different thought leaders in writing this book, one of the questions I've asked each of them is, How did you know what you knew? How did you come up with these brilliant, well-crafted, thoughtful lessons learned that you are out sharing with audiences? As you were going about your life, could you identify the "teachable moments"?

Well, no. They couldn't.

Instead they encountered many crossroads in their lives, made some horrible mistakes, and had some extraordinary triumphs—exactly like the rest of us. But some took the time to write down their experiences along the way, and others spent time reflecting on their journey afterwards. They chose to acknowledge that the challenges they faced and the opportunities that presented themselves were not just individual turning points but might be universal lessons that were worth sharing with others.

Dr. Nina Bhatti, a former Hewlett-Packard executive who is a frequent speaker about her own leadership lessons, explained to me, "When I share an aspect or a lesson that I've learned, that allows me to re-internalize it. I actually learn from myself. That moment of sharing it, beyond just your own thoughts, kind of makes you realize what it was again, what you really learned from that experience. And it sort of drives it home for you."[3]

What are some ways you can capture your lessons learned and then distill them to share with others? You can create a wisdom journal and learn to "JuxtaRows" your ideas.

Create a Wisdom Journal

Chip Conley founded Joie de Vivre Hospitality when he was twenty-six years old and grew it from one hotel into the second-largest boutique hotel company in America. He survived not one but two "once in a lifetime" downturns between 2000 and 2010 (the dot-com crash and September 11, as well as the deep recession and fiscal crisis of 2008). Yet in 2010, the company won the number one Customer Satisfaction Award in the United States from Market Metrix, beating out Marriott, Hilton, Hyatt, Sheraton, Westin, and Kimpton.[4] Along the way, Conley codified his lessons learned in four books and has given hundreds of talks around the world sharing his ideas and leadership know-how.

This all got me wondering: how does someone run a successful business and find time to write four books? I asked Conley how it all began. "In 1997," he told me, "we had thirteen different hotels, and I started to be asked to give speeches. I was thirty-six or thirty-seven at that point. The idea of going out and giving a speech—initially, I admit, it was an ego-fed proposition. Then over time it really became more of an opportunity for me to impart wisdom—and at thirty-six you know you don't have that much wisdom. But you have the ability to try to actually make sense of what your life has meant. I love that part of it. To me that is the best part of being a thought leader; it forces me to reflect on what I've learned. Then, as they say, the best teachers are great learners, and I believe that it forces me to be a great learner in order for me to be a teacher."

Along the way, he had kept a sort of private business journal. During good times, he didn't have time to jot down more than a note or two. But when things started to go in the wrong direction, or the economy dealt his company a particular blow, he took time to reflect on what was happening and document it as best he could. This became the basis for his first book, about business rebels. During the process of writing that first book, he realized, "There were really key principles that I was trying to get across, and my story was sort of the way that I could introduce those principles."

Conley was thankful to have gotten some great advice from Alan Weber, cofounder of Fast Company and former managing editor of *Harvard Business Review*. "He said, 'Before you write a book, go out and speak about it a lot; that will help you refine it down to something that is a much more manageable nugget.'" Conley learned that "the process of speaking about it actually forces you to edit it, because a group doesn't want to listen to you talk for four hours. It also forces you to understand what it is that resonates with the audience."

He has followed this process for each of his four books. He's kept a journal about his experiences, distilled his lessons learned into principles, then "went out and started talking about the subject before I ever start[ed] writing about it."[5]

How can you follow in his footsteps? Begin with a "wisdom journal."

If you already keep a journal, great! If not, at the end of the day or each week, could you set aside fifteen minutes to write down the highlights of what happened? What were the painful moments, the funny experiences, or the most challenging decisions you made? Here are a few more questions:

- What have I learned from this experience?
- What did I do well?
- What could I have done differently?
- Is there a universal lesson here that others could apply?

I realize it can be difficult to find the time (or the distance) to observe yourself. We're all in a hurry, and often we are not the best judge of what is under way, because we're in the middle of it. This is why it's essential to set aside time on a regular basis to capture circumstances and details, to articulate your experiences and lessons learned, before they slip away in the rush of life.

How do you turn your personal experiences (those captured in your wisdom journal or elsewhere) into universal principles that you can share with others?

Learn to JuxtaRows

As thought leaders, we can in fact share our experiences with the broader world, if we know how to "distill our insights into an anthology of first-of-their-kind best practices or a systematic, sequential methodology." To show you how to do that, I conferred with Intrigue Expert Sam Horn, author of *Pop!: Create the Perfect Pitch, Title, and Tagline for Anything.*[6] (Full disclosure: Sam Horn is one of my favorite mentors.) Through her award-winning books, keynotes, and her Intrigue Agency, Horn has helped dozens of authors and many thousands of entrepreneurs, business owners, and thought leaders scale their impact far beyond what they imagined possible.

Horn developed her technique "JuxtaRows" (a takeoff on the word *juxtapose*) to help people get clarity about anything. She assured me that this exercise works for any type of expertise or project, whether you are a lawyer or a banker or an inventor. It works for CEOs and nonprofit leaders, healthcare workers, and product managers. In other words, it's helpful for every thought leader who has taken the steps outlined so far in this book.

You might think that to codify your lessons learned, you will write down all the things you did right along the way. But Horn advises, "Instead, start with what didn't work. If we focus on what does work, how to do it better, how to improve it—that almost always comes out as platitudes or clichés. So we don't start there. Where we start is where we have a lot of passion and conviction—about what we've learned *doesn't* work, what sabotages performance, what compromises success."

Here are the steps in the JuxtaRows process:

1. Get a fresh piece of paper and draw a vertical line down the center.
2. Select a topic you know a lot about.
3. On the left, write two of the following: What's Wrong, What Doesn't Work, What Sabotages Success, What Compromises Performance, or What Hurts.
4. On the right, choose the two that align: What's Right, What Does Work, What Supports Success, What Supports Performance, or What Helps.
5. Start on the left, and write down as many real-life examples of what people (you or others) do wrong in this arena. Add details of exactly what you've witnessed, experienced, or done *wrong*. Add first-person dialogue whenever possible.
6. Next add examples on the right of how you've learned to do it better and of what you know to be the best practice (even if you didn't do it that way the first time).

7. Select a pithy or profound phrase from the example or dialogue and turn it into a distinctive title or name for your chapter, presentation, blog, or method.

Let me walk you through how this might work. Let's say you are a business writer and you are ready to distill what you know about great business writing (Step 2). Rather than focus on what makes someone a good writer, Horn suggests you turn it around and try to answer the opposite. Ask, "What makes someone a terrible writer—that you're just rolling your eyes, that you don't even want to read the next page?" (Step 3).

By focusing on the negative, we can really dig in and play—because we are *all* good at being critical, at poking holes in things, at finding the flaw, or telling others how *not* to do things. I could spend hours telling you how to be a bad writer, and how bad some other writers are and why. Couldn't you?

Next Horn advises you to ask yourself, "What's an example of that?" "Put me in the scene: what's a time when you were reading something and you threw the business book down in disgust, or you were reading a report and you're thinking, *This is a complete waste of time?*"

Here's an example, from one of my experiences with a client, of "What Doesn't Work" (Step 5). I was completing a quarterly review for an executive and her boss told me, "Whenever I get an email from her, I go get a cup of coffee and I settle in, because I know it's going to take at least thirty minutes to get through it." Ouch! That's definitely an example of how *not* to be a great writer.

Now let's consider the opposite. What would a great email be like? It would be short and pithy and have at the top a summary of the action needed—in other words, it could be read on the run, which is how most of us read email. We'd write those specifics of "What Does Work" over on the right side of our paper (Step 6).

Finally, figure out a unique name that best sums up your lesson learned. In this case, you might name it the "Cup of Coffee Email Rule" (Step 7), using what my client's boss said as a short-cut description that anyone would get. (You don't have time to read a cup-of-coffee email, do you?)

When you use a specific experience from your own life as the basis for a valuable lesson for everyone, you create a unique takeaway; it's something you can call your own *and* it's a universal principle. If you were sharing this advice with an audience, you could say, "Don't write a cup-of-coffee email," and it would be far more memorable than saying, "Don't write long emails." Right?

That's the goal: create lessons learned that are memorable, anchored in your own experiences, and yet universal.

Horn believes the JuxtaRows process works because "When we start with what doesn't work, it immediately pulls out more visceral, from-the-gut kinds of reactions. It's instantly more interesting. By selecting an anecdote—a real-life, first-person example—that exemplifies our point, that's also when we find our own original ideas. That's when we're engaged and it's something we haven't heard before."

She advises, "When you pull out of the first-person description and dialogue something that gives it an original name, it doesn't disappear into the text. You've captured it and leveraged it in a way that makes it memorable."[7]

Try JuxtaRows for yourself or ask a friend or colleague to do this exercise with you. Be sure to record your discussions, as you'll often uncover many hidden gems during your conversations that you'll be able to use later, during Step 7. If you have a journal or you've kept notes or calendars that document your experiences, use them to jog your memory.

One important caveat to guarantee success: stick to what you know. If you stray too far from your exact area of expertise, you will be far less compelling and far less likely to come up with those first-person stories. Also, if you have not worked alone—if you have a cofounder or a "first follower"—you might want to invite them to do the exercise with you. They will likely remember things that you have long forgotten.

In preparing to use JuxtaRows, ask yourself these questions:

- What topic and question could you select that would allow you to distill your lessons learned?
- Who could help you (colleagues, employees, board members, advisors, friends)?
- What materials do you have stored away that can jog your memory or serve as your wisdom journal for this purpose?

For many reading this chapter, the idea of capturing and distilling your lessons learned so that you can share them in a speech, document them in a video, write about them in a blog, or capture them in your own book is sufficient. If that's you, you can skip ahead now to the next chapter, where you'll learn how to "Put Yourself on S.H.O.U.T." in any number of venues.

But if you are interested in understanding the steps to turn your ideas into a framework that can become your unique intellectual property, then the rest of this chapter is for you.

CREATE YOUR INTELLECTUAL PROPERTY

I would love to argue that the best ideas always win, but we know that's not really the case. That's why advertisers and marketers are paid so much money: they help ideas stand out from the pack. If you want to clearly differentiate yourself from others in your niche and build momentum for the efforts you have under way, one of the best ways to do that is to codify your ideas into your own intellectual property.

Intellectual property (IP) is defined by the *Merriam-Webster* dictionary as "property (an idea, invention, or process) that derives from the work of the mind or intellect."[8] Why create intellectual property? Because it is something you can own and protect as your own. IP creates value for you, your team, or your organization—whoever owns the rights to that property.

Here are the steps to create intellectual property out of your methodology or framework:

1. Create a simple, preferably visual, representation that is easy to understand.
2. Clearly document how to use that framework.
3. Give it a great name.
4. Show proof that it works.
5. Protect and control its use.

Develop a Visual Representation

Not every framework, methodology, or set of best practices will lend itself to a graphic, pictorial, or visual representation, but if you can find a way to do so, you'll go a long way toward engaging followers and explaining your ideas. Most people are visual learners—they learn more quickly with their eyes than their ears. *Think of yourself as a visual storyteller: you can show as well as tell others your ideas.*

Chip Conley learned about the power of a simple image when he simplified Maslow's "Hierarchy of Needs" into "three basic themes: survival at the base, success at the middle, and transformation at the top. Applied to employees, these needs translated as money, recognition, and meaning."[9]

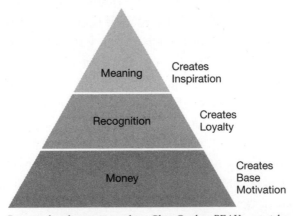

Reprinted with permission from Chip Conley, *PEAK*, copyright 2007.

He used that revised image and expanded on those basic concepts to create a much more detailed framework that guided his actions as he turned his hotel business around in the midst of a downturn.

Reprinted with permission from Chip Conley, *PEAK*, copyright 2007.

He then went on to share that larger framework in his book *PEAK: How Great Companies Get Their Mojo from Maslow* and presented his theory around the world, ensuring that his ideas spread far beyond the hotel industry.[10]

In her new role as vice chancellor of workforce development for the California Community College System, Van Ton-Quinlivan has created the "Doing What MATTERS for Jobs & the Economy Framework,"[11] which is graphically represented by a circle divided into four quadrants and a circular arrow in the center that connects each quadrant to the others. Whenever she speaks or writes about her ideas, she uses this image to call on her various partners to align together on the four related actions that make up the overall strategy she is advocating.

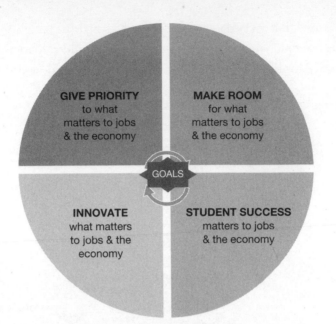

Reprinted with permission from Van Ton-Quinlivan.

After I began sharing the seven-step thought leadership frame-work that is outlined in this book, I realized I needed my own visual representation of my ideas. I hired the team at Alimat, Inc., to turn my ideas into protectable IP.[12]

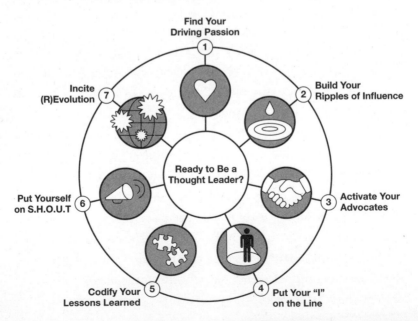

To get started in creating your own visual representation, open PowerPoint and take a look at the SmartArt menu or use your favorite search engine to look for images of frameworks or methodologies. If you are describing a repeating methodology, perhaps choose a circular image. If you're depicting a four-step process, a two-by-two matrix might work. Try to present your ideas in a variety of ways and then test those images with different people—those who already know what you're talking about, and those who don't—and see which ideas people respond to. This is an iterative process that takes tweaking.

If you can afford to, hire a good graphic artist and a talented wordsmith. Reach out to friends to get their recommendations, or use an online marketplace of designers (Elance or oDesk). Send them your first attempts and let them help you create a more memorable visual representation—one that is unique to you, which you can own and trademark.

Document Your Framework

Just as Chip and Dan Heath recommend that you "script the critical moves," you will need to clearly outline the specific, detailed steps that others should follow to replicate what you've done. While this can be a major undertaking, the payoff is enormous, as I learned when we began to codify the Springboard process and, later, the PowerPathway initiative.

In 2001, after hosting three Springboard Venture Forum events, the Springboard team—myself, Amy Millman, Kay Koplovitz, Debra Filtzer, Andrea Silbert, and a few others—decided that we knew enough to begin to document the "magic" that made our events so successful. Months of back-and-forth emails ensued as we created a "manual" that detailed how to create, fund, and host a successful Springboard program. Over the following twelve years, the manual has undergone significant edits and revisions as each new Springboard program provides its own lessons learned.

The hours of time that went into the creation (and updating) of this document have more than paid off for the organization. Springboard can now charge a license fee for their manual to other groups who want to create their own Venture Forums. Springboard has also ensured that they have intellectual property—something that is pretty rare in the nonprofit world. They've even been able to turn some of that process into online tools and systems that they can also license over time.

When Van Ton-Quinlivan first created the industry-community partnership program PowerPathway, she modeled her efforts on a similar program she had learned about in the biotech industry. She had no manual to guide her—she had to create a simple PowerPoint diagram that explained the proposed partnership model to others in her company.

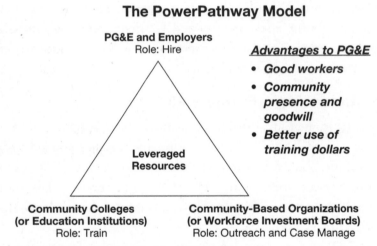

The PowerPathway Model

Reprinted with permission from Van Ton-Quinlivan.

Over time, we built out a presentation from this one slide to eight to ten slides, which represented not only the overarching framework but also the implementation plan. We then documented the bright spots as we completed the successful rollout of PowerPathway to other regions. As she began to share the PowerPathway story outside the company, Ton-Quinlivan used a version of these slides for industry talks, stakeholder meetings, and consortium presentations.

The slides were regularly updated—the model became more generalizable; the implementation plan broadened; and the bright spots were no longer exclusively within PG&E's territory but dotted across the state as others adopted the PowerPathway model.

Then we created a "train the trainer" program—a user manual and a one-day training event—to teach partners how to implement every step for rolling out a nine-month PowerPathway program. We also produced a how-to guide that was distributed, free of charge, to community partners. We revised and reframed the user manual and how-to-guide as needed to document the lessons learned and add to our script of the critical moves others should follow to replicate the PowerPathway program in their regions.

As you document your own process, start with a set of slides, write a user manual, create an annual report, or construct a project timeline. If your audience is primarily online, try a video to get your ideas across. The goal is to catalyze others by creating an easy-to-follow set of how-to steps that they can use to replicate the most important aspects of your ideas, process, or program. The easier you make it, the more likely they will be successful.

There is always a tension here between creating a generalizable process and a generic set of steps. You don't want to water everything down, but on the other hand, you do want to standardize what you can. The nuances to this may require you to get some help from an experienced knowledge management specialist or curriculum designer.

Find a Great Name

Part of creating a great brand for your intellectual property is finding a memorable name. Think back to the JuxtaRows exercise and the Cup of Coffee Email Rule. A one-of-a-kind name like that is a great start. Can you go further and come up with something catchy and memorable? Can you coin a new word (PowerPathway), adapt or adopt a word in common parlance (Springboard)?

Here are some other options:

- *Name your system or methodology after yourself.* Examples are Maslow's Hierarchy of Needs, the Suzuki Method of teaching music, and Michael Porter's Five Forces Analysis.
- *Select another famous person to name it after.* The Malcolm Baldrige quality standards were named after the U.S. Secretary of Commerce from 1981 to 1987.
- *Name it after your company.* The creators of the Cisco Networking Academy Program (discussed in Chapter Seven) found that tying their efforts to the Cisco brand was key to gaining widespread adoption.
- *Come up with a unique word or phrase that you can trademark.* When Jerry McNellis began to spread the word about his strategic planning methodology (see Chapter Seven), he registered it as Compression Planning to indicate that his process can speed up (compress) your planning time considerably.

Show Proof That It Works

In order for others to be motivated to adopt your ideas, they need to know they actually work. The Heaths encourage us to share the "bright spots"—our successes—as that encourages others to think change is possible. Measuring real impact can be challenging, but don't let that scare you off. What are the outcomes you are most proud of? How can you quantify them?

Here are some options:

- What is a measurable ROI (return on investment) that others can expect from duplicating your program?
- What significant alteration is possible in people's behavior or attitudes if they follow your framework?
- Is there an increase in the speed or accuracy in which something is accomplished if they use your methodology?

- Was there an unexpected improvement in the way things have always been done because of ideas you introduced?

At FWE, one of our goals was to increase the amount of venture capital funding that was raised by women-founded and women-led companies; thus we tracked funding received and jobs created by the members of our organization. Our other goal was to increase awareness of the issue of women's access to venture funding, so we also tracked media mentions and the opportunities we had to spread our message—speeches given, articles written about our work, and audiences reached.

When she started the PowerPathway program, Van Ton-Quinlivan wanted to increase the diversity of newly hired employees. Thus, she developed an annual report card that tracked the diversity statistics of those hired within the industry that had completed the PowerPathway program versus those that had not, in order to show the program's impact. As the program's statistics improved, she gained more and more followers to her ideas and more people willing to replicate the PowerPathway programs in their own regions.

As you develop your own proof points, tie the metrics you are tracking to the goals you set out to achieve. Your metrics can even be qualitative, as long as they are in some way *measurable, verifiable, and actionable*—proof of what really happened, inspiration for others, and guidelines for what they too will need to track to build on your early wins. (And no, before you ask, don't shade the truth, even a little bit. Your credibility is at stake here. If you are going to create a movement, others have to believe that you've taken the first steps and shown them the way.)

Protect and Control Your IP

Thought leaders often overlook this. Several of the people I interviewed for this book spoke to me about their experience with others who wittingly or unwittingly stole their ideas, hard work, phraseology, methodologies, and so on. Don't be naïve and think it could never happen to you. It does and it might.

Whenever possible, safeguard your intellectual property—specifically the name, methodology, and frameworks—with legal protection. I am not a lawyer, so I recommend that you get actual legal advice; but trademarks, copyrights, and patents each can be used in different situations to certify that others do not take your original ideas for their own. The latest model, regularly adopted by thought leaders, in addition to their copyright, is a Creative Commons license.[13]

Creative Commons (CC) is a nonprofit that provides free, easy-to-use licenses that allow you to give the public permission to use your work; you set the conditions of use. Again, these licenses only take effect when a work is copyrighted, so read the fine print. Do pay attention to these guidelines when you are building on *others'* work that is protected by a CC license. You may have the right to reproduce and distribute others' works, or you may not.

Fortunately everything you've learned in this chapter about creating a unique name and a documented methodology will help you ensure that your ideas are accurately labeled as yours. Keep written proof of what you have created and the date you developed it. This will be required as proof of your ownership if you decide to seek copyright or trademark protection.

Once you've protected your intellectual property, you will also need to decide if you want to sell, license, or give away the rights to reuse it. We'll cover this further in Chapter Seven, but the most difficult decisions in the early stages are what you will control and what you won't. When Ton-Quinlivan began encouraging others to replicate the PowerPathway program, she was very careful about which programs were branded with the PowerPathway name and which were not. When Springboard began licensing the Venture Forum programs to others, they made dozens of decisions about what they wanted to control: pricing, numbers of presenters, types of companies selected. In each case, the final decision was made less for reasons of consistency than it was to ensure a high-quality brand experience for anyone attending or participating in the programs.

Before you give someone the right to use your brand, make sure that you outline exactly what you're agreeing to. And as you create your first agreements for others to replicate your programs or ideas, the more clarity you can establish about what is required from both parties, the better. (Often you can model these agreements on others. Reach out to those in your network who have example templates. Or find a lawyer who specializes in franchise agreements. They are often the best experts in this sort of planning.) Then leave the door open for feedback and dispute resolution. These are a natural part of any relationship.

Now that you have created a memorable, repeatable, measureable, verifiable, actionable, and protectable framework, it's time to be out sharing it with the world. What you do next will depend greatly on your intended audience. That's why we're going to spend the whole next chapter talking about how to "Put Yourself on S.H.O.U.T." And then in Chapter Seven we'll discuss how to amplify and accelerate your efforts to scale real change in the world.

Before we move on, I want to mention the many experts out there who can help you distill your lessons learned and turn them into a workable framework. These might include a curriculum designer, instructional design expert, knowledge management specialist, or even a ghostwriter or book coach. These folks gather at organizations like the ASTD (American Society for Training and Development), KMPro (Knowledge Management Professional Society), the National Speakers Association, and the Authors Guild. Ask someone you know for a recommendation—often large companies have a whole team of people with this expertise. Check LinkedIn or ask those on your personal board of directors for their advice on where to turn.

CODIFY YOUR LESSONS LEARNED: A QUICK REVIEW

In this step of the thought leadership journey, successful thought leaders

- Begin a wisdom journal or store mementos along the way
- Use exercises like "JuxtaRows" to distill their insights into a set of guiding principles or lessons learned they can share with the world
- Create intellectual property: represent their ideas visually; add a creative and memorable name and a clear set of instructions for what needs to be done to repeat their success
- Devise verifiable metrics and collect proof points that document their progress to date and support their ideas
- Protect their intellectual property with a trademark, copyright, patent, or other legal protection
- Decide what they'd like to control and what they will not control
- Hire needed expertise, such as knowledge management experts or a ghostwriter, to move this phase along to completion

MORE FOOD FOR THOUGHT

Get Your Book Written

Many people who call Thought Leadership Lab are eager to write a book, but few are excited about taking a year or more to complete the process. That's why I was excited to learn about a technique for writing a book using a relatively straightforward interview method. The truth is, I used a form of this technique myself; I just wasn't quite as organized and smart about it as I would have been if I'd heard about this method before I started.

Try the Interview Technique

I've long admired Dr. Tina Seelig, the executive director for the Stanford Technology Ventures Program, the entrepreneurship center at Stanford University's School of Engineering. She has authored sixteen popular science books and educational games and offers an amazing MOOC—massive open online course—in creativity, which I recommend highly.[14]

Seelig shared with me the technique she now uses for writing her books. "I start by writing an outline of the book," she told me. "Then, I compile a list of a few dozen people that I want to interview. Over a few weeks, I set up lunches or meetings with each of these people. During my conversations with them, I take a lot of handwritten notes. When I get back to my office, I review the notes and circle the ideas that seem to resonate and fit with my outline. Just before I go to bed, I review these circled ideas." After she percolates on those ideas overnight while she sleeps, she gets up in the morning and types up the interview, and then starts all over again with another lunchtime get-together.

(continued)

When she has completed all the interviews, she has a lot of great content for her book. She weaves it all together with her own ideas to create bestsellers like *inGenius: A Crash Course on Creativity*,[15] which shares hundreds of real-life examples of entrepreneurs, executives, and investors who use creativity every day in their work.[16]

Lest you think this can only work for Stanford professors, who have a wide network, let me assure you that people around the globe, even those you don't know, are eager to share their stories and ideas with you—if you just ask. I was amazed at how many people generously shared their experiences with me as part of the creation of this book. Draft a courteous note explaining why you'd like to interview them, or find someone who can send a note on your behalf. Not one person I reached out to turned me away, and I'm guessing you'll have the same experience.

CHAPTER 6

PUT YOURSELF ON S.H.O.U.T.

Now that you have claimed your niche, started your first ripples, activated your advocates, and identified and codified your lessons learned, it's time to create a far-reaching network of friends, fans, and followers that will spread the word about your activities.

To amplify the impact and influence of your ideas and leave a legacy that matters, you are now ready to put yourself on S.H.O.U.T.: Select your audience and venue, Hone your message, Overcome resistance, Understand potential pitfalls, and Transform individuals into a community.

"OK," you may be saying, "I want to 'put myself on S.H.O.U.T.' but do I have to tweet? I don't have time for that. Do I have to speak? I hate public speaking. Do I need to write a book? I'm not very good at writing."

The truth is, you don't *have* to tweet or speak or write. You can keep doing what you've been doing: working hard to change the world. You can put your head down, focus on the next activity on your to-do list, and a month from now or a year from now or a decade from now, you might be ready to take the next step to be a thought leader.

Or you could get going now. You decide.

Perhaps before I show you how to S.H.O.U.T. for yourself, I can inspire you to get started if I share the story of Avinash Kaushik, digital marketing evangelist at Google, who learned that he could be a widely known and recognized thought leader even with a family and a demanding full-time job.

CASE STUDY: AVINASH KAUSHIK, GOOGLE

Avinash Kaushik had a surprising moment when his eight-year-old son came to him and asked, "Daddy, are you famous?" It turns out his son had found his listing on Wikipedia and for the first time realized his dad might just "be somebody." At times, I'm guessing, Kaushik is as surprised as his son that today his blog, "Occam's Razor," is no longer an obscure, online how-to guide for web analytics geeks. It is now read not only by Fortune 10 chief marketing officers but also by people from Botswana to Borneo. He also has over 100,000 followers of his Twitter feed and 150,000 in his Google+ community.

It all began when Kaushik, then the director of web research and analytics at the accounting software company Intuit, was invited to speak at a small industry conference. Following his talk, two influential industry leaders invited him to think about writing a blog. Over the next few months, Kaushik did his homework, researching extensively and reading other blogs. He remembers being influenced by Guy Kawasaki's "blogging principles," which encouraged him to think of his blog as a way to give back.[1] He told me, "I have learned a lot from others, and my hope with my blog is to share back with the world, to the extent that I can, in my core area of expertise." He also learned to "Think *book*, not *diary*" and accordingly chose to write less often and more thoughtfully, in a way that added real value for his readers.

For the first ninety days, Kaushik wrote a practice blog exclusively for his team and his wife, getting their feedback before taking the blog to a wider audience. He was quite hesitant to "put himself out there" as an expert. He also had no idea whether he could actually write regularly enough for a blog while doing a full-time and very hectic job.

From the first, he decided, "I'm going to be different. There were already a hundred blogs in analytics by the time I started writing. They were established thought leaders. They had books published. I didn't let that overwhelm me or deter me. I said, 'I'm going to cover a point of view and I'm going to start putting it out there. I'm going to say things that other people don't think about or say.'"

He began by posting twice a week, writing from 10 P.M. until 12:30 A.M., after the kids went to bed. From the beginning, he was amazed that each of his blog posts received numerous comments from his readers. "My blog was one of the first that was written by somebody who was actually inside a company who was doing this work. It has this strong smell of reality. I didn't want anything from anybody. I wanted to share my lessons learned that you will find helpful if you're a practitioner."

Six months later he got a call from John Wiley & Sons asking him to compile the posts into a book. Since he had two small children by then, he "negotiated" with his wife, and his boss, to set aside the time needed to complete the book. He wrote every weekend in his office from 8 A.M. to 6 P.M. for about ten weeks, taking his existing blog posts and then adding 50 percent more to "fill in the holes." He learned to love long airplane flights because they gave him more time to write.

Kaushik admits, "It is an awful lot of effort and work, especially if you're working full-time. Unless you're truly passionate about it, unless it motivates you at a very deep level, unless somehow you find the sense of pride or accomplishment, you will never ever be successful." Regardless, he is not sorry he made the effort—in fact, his book and his blog have put him on an amazing trajectory.

Receiving a promotion to senior manager and then director, Kaushik was given the resources to build his internal Intuit team to thirty people before being recruited to work at Google. There he created his own job description and has since been promoted to be the company's digital marketing evangelist. His book *Web Analytics: An Hour a Day* was the top seller for its imprint and has been published in seven languages. He has since written a second book, *Web Analytics 2.0*, and continues to speak widely, for high fees.

Throughout, Kaushik has always focused his blog posts (and his books) on helping others who face the same challenges that he faces every day. He codifies the solutions and best practices that he and his team have discovered. His mantra for writing is, "I will only write a blog post if it has something incredible of value to offer." Today he writes about once every two weeks.

And although he admits that he never liked to read others' books when he first started out (preferring to figure things out for himself), he found he enjoys the process of writing easy-to-approach and highly useful books. Intuit, too, was happy about his blog from the beginning, "because it allowed them to become a very strong brand in this space." The HR team told him that his efforts to heighten their brand helped them recruit new talent to Intuit. It was a win-win situation.

His own satisfaction comes too from the email he gets from his readers. "At first, I would get email every once in awhile. Now, once a day there's somebody writing me who says, 'You helped me find my career.'" Kaushik told me, "You can imagine the quiet sense of joy that brings to you. Just joy. That has made me more motivated to write and share."

His other reward has been the opportunity to become a philanthropist. When he received his first small advance from Wiley, even though he and his wife did not have much money they decided to donate the entire check to charity. They followed that tradition for all the monies earned from both books. He takes a lot of personal satisfaction from the fact that over the last few years the success of his blog and his books has allowed him and his wife to donate over a quarter million dollars to their charities. Kaushik knows that without the platform he has developed, he would never have had the chance to make as large an impact in the arenas that he cares about.[2]

I think you'll agree that Kaushik's career and personal S.H.O.U.T. trajectory have been remarkable, but what I like about his story is that he started small and built his friends, fans, and followers bit by bit using a blog, speaking, and eventually a book—all while building a successful career. When you are ready, here's how you can do the same.

<u>S</u>ELECT YOUR AUDIENCE AND VENUE

No matter whether you choose to write, speak, or use social media, it is a good idea to take the time to study others' successes before jumping in, play the small venues first, and make sure that you are building a high-quality personal brand.

Study Others' Successes

When you set out to S.H.O.U.T. for the first time (PR, blogging, social media, public speaking, testifying in front of a legislative committee), look around you for successful role models and study up before you get started. Not only will you identify best practices to follow; you'll likely also find things that you can improve on.

Avinash Kaushik took several weeks to monitor popular blogs in his and other industries before he got started. Then he read the advice from successful bloggers on what to do and not to do and experimented with a practice blog for a few trusted colleagues.

Here are some places to find successful role models:

- Read top-rated blogs in your field to learn which are receiving the most followership and comments (refer to Alltop[3] or Technorati[4]).

- Watch some videos of well-reviewed speakers to see how they connect with their audience (explore YouTube or the National Speakers Association site).
- Review some recent best-selling lists to see what is selling now.

Play the Small Venues First

No matter where you choose to begin, it's always a good idea to start small and ask for help. As my friend Dr. Nina Bhatti, CEO of Kokko, Inc., and a very popular speaker at association and conference events, advises, "Like a comedian, you want to play the small venues first, then take your best material to the larger arenas." Look at each of your early events as "auditions" and imagine that there is always a "scout" in the audience who can "lead you to the next venue."[5]

This advice is equally applicable for those who choose to spread the word about their activities through writing, using social media, or launching a YouTube channel. Van Ton-Quinlivan first shared the PowerPathway story on a panel at a small local conference where she knew most of the attendees. Zoe Dunning first spoke at a small political rally, and Miki Agrawal found a ready audience for her entrepreneurial story among high school students. Only after honing their ideas did they take them to a larger stage.

Before you venture onto a stage for the first time or submit your first guest blog, reach out to someone who has taken the path before you and get some advice. Don't be discouraged if the first time you try for something (like a speaking opportunity) you aren't selected. There will be other chances. As you continue to build your thought leadership profile, others will begin to seek *you* out and then you'll be able to be choosy. Prioritize those opportunities that focus on friendly audiences, where you will get a chance to test out your ideas.

In "More Food for Thought" at the end of this chapter, you'll find lots of ideas for potential S.H.O.U.T. venues, but here are a few to get you started:

- Find a small industry event—a panel or a roundtable—and ask to be invited.

- Host a brown-bag lunch or open house to share what your team is working on.
- Identify a local organization that might value learning more about what's going on in their area, and look for a chance to present.
- Look for advice from other people you know who are frequent speakers or bloggers or tweeters.

Build a Quality Personal Brand

Early in my career, I never realized that an individual could or should have a personal brand. Then Fast Company published Tom Peters's article "The Brand Called You," and suddenly self-branding was everywhere.[6] For those who don't want to dig up the article (although it's well worth reading), here's how Peters defines brand: "A brand is a promise of the value you'll receive." That clarifies it, doesn't it? Well, not really.

Let me approach this from a different angle. If you were to turn on your TV and close your eyes, you would pretty quickly tell whether it was the *Ellen DeGeneres Show* or the *Martha Stewart Show* by the type of content that was being discussed, as well as the word choice, inflection, tone, and pace. Now imagine you could see the screen but not hear the words. You would certainly tell the difference between the studio set for Jon Stewart versus David Letterman even if neither host was visible on your TV screen.

If someone comes to watch you speak, if they visit your site or read what you wrote, they should know that they didn't walk onto the wrong set by accident. You want to create your own one-of-a-kind brand "personality." For example, if you position your brand as straight talk, people will come to rely on you to give them the real scoop. If you are the curmudgeon, like Lewis Black, then run with that. Some prefer quiet and humble; others are bold and provocative. Kaushik's point of view was, "I'm going to say things that other people don't think about or say." He focused on providing the practitioner's point of view. This allowed him to stand out and quickly get known in his niche, since no one could confuse his blog with anything else that was out there.[7]

Beyond just words, you will stand out further when you develop a distinctive visual identity—a logo or a style of writing that is uniquely yours. You might also choose a personal trademark, like Scott Ginsberg, the Nametag Guy, who has spent over 4,500 days wearing a nametag.[8] However you go about it, ensure that your personal brand is distinctive and your point of view is clear, well defined, and consistent, as that helps people decide whether they want to be part of your tribe. The best brand reputation for a thought leader is being knowable, likeable, and trustable,[9] being someone who provides value to others.

It is never too early to think about your brand. If you don't actively manage your reputation, you may inadvertently create one that doesn't serve you. There may already be assumptions out there about you or your chosen field which you will need to overcome (accountants are dull, entrepreneurs are stubborn, and scientists are wonky—right?). If you understand these preconceived notions, you will have the option of playing to the stereotype or surprising your audience with your ability to play against type.

A lot goes into creating a trusted brand. Above all, it's about taking out any bad surprises (by ensuring consistency in look, attitude, and style; fact-checking anything you put out in the world; crediting your sources; disclosing any connections that might lead to a conflict of interest) and leaving in the good surprises (over-delivering value; offering unexpected insights; being open about when you've made a mistake). To learn more about branding, read one of the dozens of books on the subject, such as *The Brand You 50* by Tom Peters,[10] or *Me 2.0* by Dan Schawbel.[11]

- Develop a "point of view" that others will identify as uniquely yours. Will you be folksy and approachable? Knowledgeable and wise? Bold and to the point?
- Create a visually strong and unique brand identity (color, logo, icon, tagline) that aligns to this point of view. (Make sure to

align to your organization's brand guidelines if there are any.) If this is not your area of expertise, hire someone to design your materials. Find designers on Elance.com or run a logo contest on 99designs.com.

- Use this brand everywhere (marketing materials, website, opening screen of your YouTube video, Facebook page, and so on).
- Always, always, always create value for your chosen community.

HONE YOUR MESSAGE

Your success as a thought leader is predicated on your ability to engage others by honing your message and telling a great story. This could be your own story or the story of your "customers." You could tell that story with data, text, or visuals. You could present it in a blog, tweet, or a Facebook post. You could write a book or a monthly column. Regardless, it all starts with a well-crafted story.

Learn to Tell a Great Story

Our ability to command attention and respect is fairly directly correlated to our ability to write well, speak clearly, and tell stories that engage others and make them care. According to Jennifer Aaker, professor of marketing at Stanford Business School, studies show that stories are significantly more memorable than facts alone.[12]

Few are born with the gift of storytelling—the rest of us have to work to develop it. Intrigue Expert and author Sam Horn has many wonderful storytelling techniques in her books and on her blog, but my favorite is one she calls the "empathy telescope."[13] As she explains, when we focus on one individual's story, we can engage our audience's empathy and motivate them to get involved. (Take a look at Horn's YouTube video, where she explains this far better than I can.[14])

We can't get our arms around such issues as world hunger or childhood poverty. They are simply too big. It is by focusing your attention on one child, Horn teaches, that you can engage people to care and act. Groups like Save the Children do this to great effect. We can learn from their success when we craft our own "empathy telescope" stories, which highlight an individual rather than trying to engage people in a problem too big for them to understand or a future too far off for them to care about.

- Identify a way to use the "empathy telescope" technique to get people passionate about your issue.
- Develop your public speaking skills by attending Toastmasters, media or spokesperson training, a storytelling conference, or an improv workshop, or by hiring a private instructor.

Tell *Your* Story

Those who join your "tribe" want to identify with you—they want to understand what motivates you. The more clearly you can articulate your story and draw your audience in to identify with you, the more likely you are to build a loyal tribe. This doesn't mean sharing all your secrets, but it does mean opening up so people can get to know the real you.

When I first began to talk to the press about why I had cofounded the Forum for Women Entrepreneurs, I never thought to tell people my own story. I didn't tell them that what had motivated me was my own experience, at the age of twenty-six, of starting my first company. I never let on that as a newbie entrepreneur I had felt isolated and unprepared and that even though I'd made a lot of money, I had also made a lot of mistakes. Looking back, I'm sure those disclosures would have added to my credibility rather than detracting from it.

The truth is that your own story, particularly your own "hero's journey"—how you overcame obstacles and found your way—is what allows people to relate to you. Once they recognize that you have overcome adversity, they are more likely to believe what you say and take your advice or align with your point of view.

- What part of your own personal story are you willing to share?
- How does your past inform your efforts to bring about the *What If?* future you envision?

Tell Your "*Customers*'" Stories

In addition to *your* story, the other messages that will add value to your tribe are your "customers'" stories (feel free to replace "customers" with students, employees, clients, patients, and so on, depending on whom you work with). Share and detail the success stories of those who have tried your methodology, participated in your programs, or learned from your guiding principles.

My friend Amy Millman is the master at this sort of "shout-out." Amy and I have been partners in women's entrepreneurial initiatives ever since we came together to cofound the Springboard Venture Forums back in 1999. Since then, under Amy's remarkable leadership, Springboard has scaled from three conferences in the United States in its first year, to having a significant global impact on women's entrepreneurship.[15] In twelve years, over five hundred women have been accepted into what is now a prestigious three-month accelerator program for their businesses. As a result of the education they receive, the connections they make, and the doors that are opened for them, participating businesses have raised over $6.2 billion and counting.

In the Springboard newsletter, Amy is all about singing the praises of the people in the community—she toots everyone's horn in such a positive way that you can't help but thrill in their successes.[16] Taking the time to shout out about others is one of the roles of thought leadership—it's good messaging and good leadership.

- Whose stories can you share that best exemplify your community's success?
- What best practices do these stories exemplify?
- How can you institute the "shout-out" as one of your best practices?

Let *Them* Tell Their Stories

"You should never underestimate the potential of any passionate community united around beliefs, commonalities or shared interests," says Dave Kerpen in his book *Likeable Social Media*. Kerpen tells the story of the children's shoe brand, Stride Rite, which created an online community of moms on Facebook. In only a few years, the site had over 150,000 fans, most of them young moms. The conversation is about shoes, but it's also about kids—lots of pictures and videos of babies' first steps. The moms "help each other out with lots of baby- and child-rearing questions that have nothing to do with shoes," Kerpen continues. "Moms feel empowered, engaged, and proud to be part of the Stride Rite community."[17]

- How can you engage your community to share their stories with one another?
- How can you create a welcome place where your tribe can support one another?

Include Data as Proof Points

Often data help tell a story. What percentage improvement did your programs or ideas bring about? What impact did your actions have? You don't want to overwhelm your audience with data, but a few strategic charts or infographics can help people see what progress has been made. Publicly tracking your data over time also establishes your transparency and builds your credibility. Include this data on a website, in an annual report card, in your speeches, and in your PowerPoint pitch. But don't rely solely on data to tell your story. The real lives behind the data are far more memorable.

- Which data tell your story? How can you depict such data visually?
- Is there an infographics specialist who can help you tell your data story? (Hint: Find a freelancer online at 99 Designs or Elance.)

Pictures, Pictures, Pictures

Want to get remembered? "Draw simple pictures," advises DePaul University adjunct professor Mike Saporito. "People remember what they see longer than what they hear. Pictures carry a ton of meaning. Stop being self-conscious and draw your ideas. You'll be surprised how the drawing process creates mutual understanding."[18] In addition to drawings, add any image that tells your story. Photographs, graphic recordings, illustrations, avatars, slideshows, animation, comics, film, and video can all add to your audience engagement.

Nancy Duarte, founder and CEO of Duarte Design, a Silicon Valley-based company that helps executives create great presentations (250,000 and counting), believes, "One of the best ways to tell a story is through images. Keep in mind who the audience is and what you want them to think, feel and do when you're done. Then choose a visual tool that's most effective to convey your idea."[19]

- How can you use pictures—in all their forms—to tell your story?
- Can you hire a visual storyteller, graphic recorder, or illustrator to help you tell your story in pictures?

Frame Your Keywords

Your path to thought leadership is tied to your ability to be identified with a set of ideas and a particular niche or niches. Look back to Chapter One when you identified three overlapping circles in your Venn diagram to arrive at your thought leadership intersection point. You want to hone your message to encapsulate the keywords and phrases that best link you to your chosen circles. It helps to begin with the future in mind. Thinking ahead to one or three years from now, what are the five to ten keywords or phrases that you hope others will be able to identify as "yours"?

Some of these may be words you've coined or word combinations you've begun to use to best describe your *What If?* future. Others might be contrary views or countervailing ideas that make you stand out. They may be the name of your framework, steps in your methodology, words you've trademarked, or the name of your organization. In any case, focus your writing and speaking to introduce and reinforce these keywords. In the next chapter, we'll talk about how to monitor to see if your efforts are on track.

- Use a free service like Twitter Search, WordStream's Keyword tool or the Google Keyword Planner (Google AdWords account required) to identify potential keywords.
- Search Facebook, Twitter, or YouTube for other thought leaders in your niche and study what keywords they are using.
- Look at the submission tags for recent conferences where people get to vote for their chosen sessions—what are the tags for the sessions that are winning the most votes?

Tell Your Story Online

A 2010 study found that an overwhelming majority of reporters and editors rely on social media when researching their stories. Anyone who wants to become a key influencer needs to be active online.[20] Yet there are so many online venues, and they morph so quickly; I've included a few of the long-standing options below. You'll find more detail on my website.[21]

Start with a Web Presence   The easiest way to be discoverable online is through a personal website or LinkedIn. If you don't control what appears on your company's website, it's easy to create your own site or a LinkedIn page. (Note: Before beginning, do find out if your organization permits such activities.)

To get started on LinkedIn, search for others with your job title, skills, and interests and study how they have created their profile before beginning your own. LinkedIn highlights thought leaders in a variety of industries—they often have excellent profiles to review.[22] In your profile, highlight not only your background but also your thought leadership activities. Add as many keywords as possible. Enhance your profile with a high-quality, close-up, professional photo and a concise and compelling (not bland!) bio. Include links to your speaking schedule, blog, articles, videos, PowerPoint pitch, or any other materials you have that tell your story.

Establish your presence online:

- Develop a great bio that shares your expertise, credentials, and your unique point of view; also prepare a short version (100 words or less) to use with every blog post or article.
- Contribute guest blog posts to well-respected blogs; this is the single best way to get noticed. Larger sites pick up high-quality content from smaller sites all the time.[23]
- Use WordPress.com or Google Sites to create your own blog and website.
- Use your keywords in your LinkedIn page, and the titles of every article or blog you write and every speech you give, throughout your website or LinkedIn page.

Add Social Media   Once you are ready to step onto a larger stage, you will want to consider social media. If you have been online forever, you can skip this section. For the rest of you, here is a quick overview of the top online options. Again, you'll find more details on my website.

Twitter is great for real-time updating about your activities and for finding out what's of the moment or part of the meme. You can follow other thought leaders and explore what they are saying and add your ideas to the online conversation. Each community has its own popular keywords (known as "hashtags"). As you follow others, you'll discover which hashtags appear most frequently and you can then begin to use those in your own tweets. Many journalists find sources on Twitter, so this is a great way to make yourself "discoverable" to those who are interested in learning more about you and the topics about which you are knowledgeable.

On *Facebook*, create a page about your activities, organization, or methodology (this page is separate from any personal page). This can become the place where others can follow you and find out what new activities you have coming up. It is also a great place to create an engaged online fan club, where your followers can share ideas, events, and questions. Tie your Facebook page to your other online content with a consistent visual identity, hashtags, and point of view.

On *Google+* you can find a like-minded group of people who are passionate about what you're passionate about. You can readily host interactive gatherings—complete with video-conferencing capabilities—with invited guest speakers. Anyone can join as an observer to watch and listen to the conversation. For thought leaders who are interested in growing their followers, Google+ is well designed for finding people who know about and want to learn about and share information on almost any topic. It's also a great place to host ongoing classes or events in your niche. Google+ is also a great place to learn about the power of visuals. Experiment with the different level of connection you can create by using great photos in your posts. Once you've identified images that resonate, you can migrate those over to a Pinterest page and create an even broader following.

Don't Forget Video   If you want to expand beyond words to video, YouTube and Vimeo are great platforms where you can create and host your own channel. The good news: video equipment costs keep going down. The bad news: so much video is being uploaded every day that you have to be more creative than taping yourself as a simple talking head to get noticed. Explore how others are using YouTube and "vlogs" (video blogs) to expand their thought leadership before you get started.

Jonathan Field, founder of the Good Life Project, first inspired me to think about the power of video as the single best way to engage people with your ideas.[24] As an experiment, I uploaded a forty-second video to my Facebook page, which got an enormous response from my followers—far more than I'd received from any previous post, even one with a great photo. After that, I was a convert. Try it and see. When you're ready to go further, Tim Ferris has written a great blog post on how to create a viral video—complete with lots of useful resources.[25]

Review the following resources to get up-to-speed on social media:

- *The Dragonfly Effect* by Jennifer Aaker[26]; *The New Relationship Marketing* by Mari Smith[27]; *What the Plus!: Google+ for the Rest of Us* by Guy Kawasaki[28]; Avinash Kaushik's blog, "Occam's Razor."[29]
- Use tools like HootSuite to more efficiently manage your social media.
- Seek out search engine optimization (SEO) tools like Moz, or try some of Google's free tools (search for Google SEO Starter Guide).
- Take a class in all the latest social media online at Market Motive[30] or at your local community college.

To Blog or Not to Blog

The first person I know who became a thought leader through the success of her blog was Beth Blecherman, who launched her "Techmamas" blog in 2005. Over the next few years, she built a loyal following of parents who were interested in her savvy advice on what she calls "Family Tech"—technology and social media for families. This led to invitations to present at conferences, write articles for technology magazines, consult with companies developing products for her target market, and write a book, *The Parent Plan*.

As her following increased, she was named to Nielsen's Power Mom 50 Influencers list, Parents Magazine Power Mom list, and Working Mother's list of Most Powerful Moms in Social Media, among other honors. Today she has an even broader reach with over 25,000 followers on Twitter and a regular following for her postings on Mashable (the largest independent online news site dedicated to covering digital culture, social media, and technology).[31]

When people ask me whether they should start a blog, I often think of Beth. Yet the world has changed a lot since 2005. Today it is both easier and more difficult to build a following for a new blog.

Easier, as there are far more channels to get the word out about what you're doing; more difficult, as there is far more competition for eyeballs and attention than ever before.

If you are considering starting a blog, it is easy to get stopped by the overwhelm factor and those inner voices: How can I possibly compete? How can I find the time? How can I be sure that anyone is listening? What if I say something that is inaccurate or controversial? Rather than stop before you start, I recommend that you just start. Stick to your thought leadership niche, write content of value to those in that niche, and do your best to write with some consistency. Position yourself as a credible source with timely, interesting, and reliable content. Your blog will increase your discoverability and may lead to an invitation to write—either as a guest blogger or a regular "columnist"—for a well-trafficked site. If you can secure an invitation to write for a popular blog in your industry or become a regular contributor to your company's blog, do so. That will likely lead to bigger opportunities, for you will build your reputation as a subject-matter expert and a key influencer.

Tell Your Story Through the Press

Getting press is usually a matter of starting local and then scaling from there. For a press release or when pitching a story, you are more likely to receive coverage if your information, program, or project is unique, fun, timely, provocative, unusual, tied to overcoming an injustice, or a "local boy or girl makes good" story. If you can tie your activities to a trend or a major news event, or provide a "scoop," you are also more likely to get traction. Bloggers and journalists who are seeking ready content often pick up press releases verbatim.[32] While this conduct may not lead to the most accurate reporting, it does give you the chance to position your story as you want it to be told.

Having an understanding of the press and having participated in spokesperson training were both hugely beneficial to my career. In 1999, when we prepared to host the first Springboard Venture

Conference, I hired a local PR firm and got their advice on how to pitch what was unique about what we were doing and how to be prepared when the press called.

And call they did. A story in our local paper, the *San Jose Mercury News*, snowballed into national coverage on radio and TV and in newspapers and magazines, including NPR, *Fast Company*, *Inc. Magazine*, and the *Wall Street Journal*.

As I learned then, local press is often the seed that starts others blooming, as reporters regularly pick up on each other's stories to write their own. Press can also add legitimacy for what you're doing. In my case, the press we received led to new sponsors, more funding for the entrepreneurs involved in the program, and more women applying for future programs. We broadened our ecosystem and I received many more invitations to speak, which allowed me to plant more seeds around the world.

Another way to become a press source is to subscribe to the HARO (Help a Reporter Out) service. Founded by PR expert Peter Shankman, HARO connects journalists working on stories with people they can quote as "experts" in those stories. While it may be challenging to keep up with the daily HARO emails asking for needed expertise, this is an excellent way for new and experienced thought leaders to become trusted resources and get noticed in their niche.[33]

One thing I learned from my days in the media spotlight: how you treat the media will often correlate to how you are treated in return. If you are highly responsive and quotable and provide needed resources and referrals to journalists, you will get a call back. If you prove yourself a reliable influencer in your niche with the top reporters and radio and TV hosts, the number of press opportunities you'll receive will likely astonish you.

Get on Stage

Throughout your thought leadership journey, it is likely you'll be invited to speak—first within your organization, then within your industry, and eventually at larger venues. As you become better known, it's likely you'll be invited more and more regularly to share your thoughts and expertise with the world. If you're already getting bombarded, see "More Food for Thought" at the end of the chapter, where I have included some criteria you can use for selecting which invitations to accept.

If you are not getting regular invitations, you can seek them out by submitting proposed topics to conference organizers or by looking online and responding to calls for proposals. Craft a thoughtful session summary and outline what topics your session will answer. Add your bio and a list of venues where you have spoken previously. If you have testimonials from previous programs, a sprinkling of those can help turn the tide in your favor—particularly if you have video testimonials from previous attendees at your programs.

If you don't yet have the name recognition to secure your own session, reach out to others with complementary expertise and propose a topic you might all weigh in on at an upcoming event. As a former conference organizer myself, I know that if you can bring in prestigious panelists, event organizers will frequently agree to let you serve as the moderator for a panel, even if you're relatively unknown. Don't hesitate to confer with the organizers to learn which topics they might want to cover where you or those in your network might have expertise.

Use each of these opportunities to improve your speaking skills and build your confidence. And stay in touch with those who book speakers so that the following year you will be invited back. Whenever possible, add photos or videos of your onstage appearances to your website, Twitter feed, or Facebook page. To further showcase your expertise, share the slides from your presentation through SlideShare and on your LinkedIn profile.

Feeling a little hesitant about all of these options for putting yourself on S.H.O.U.T.? That's what we'll cover next.

<u>O</u>VERCOME RESISTANCE

One of the most common questions I hear from clients is, "How can I find the time to blog or speak or tweet, and still do my day job?" I advise that you think about these sorts of activities as part of (rather than separate from) your job—call it the "outbound marketing part." Think back to Chapter Four and the "risk–respect feedback loop." That's what you're looking for here. As you take another risk, you'll be increasing the respect you'll receive and the impact you can have as a result.

Start small and find the activities that satisfy you, that you are good at and will keep you motivated. Learn to practice strategic ubiquity, start with twenty-minute increments, overcome any fears of the online world, pledge yourself to be in service to others, learn to overcome objections, and commit to spreading happiness.

Practice Strategic Ubiquity

No two paths from leader to thought leader are the same. You can choose to speak, write, launch a video, or put together a teleseminar series. And while I love options, the downside is that they make our audience more fragmented—and may make us more frantic as we try to keep up.

There are people who preach using every single social tool out there to reach everyone in your ecosystem. But that's just not possible. I suggest you practice "strategic ubiquity": identify the two or three platforms where your audience lives or where you can have the most impact with your message, and stick to those. Repurpose your content as much as possible. For example, if you have a blog or email newsletter, select the highlights for your social media platforms. If you like to speak, write a blog post that highlights each of your major points. Reuse your images and infographics liberally. Even if you're not an expert on using social media tools, you *can* make a difference and still do your day job.

Take Twenty Minutes Only

Overwhelmed? Use the twenty-minute-only rule. Ask those you respect where they hang out online and then spend twenty minutes a day monitoring those platforms to see how you can contribute. Do you have a talk coming up? Spend twenty minutes a day thinking about what you'll say or crafting a PowerPoint presentation. Scan your wisdom journal or review your JuxtaRows exercise to find your lessons learned, and then spend twenty minutes writing a short blog post that shares one idea.

Interview a subject-matter expert over coffee one day and write up what you learned the next. Apply for an award in your industry or community, or get someone else to nominate you. Winning an award can be a great way to increase your discoverability. Once you've tried a few different activities, see which ones you most enjoy (or get the most positive feedback from over time), and then do more of that.

Not Online—And Not Interested

I'm going to speak for a moment just to the folks who are still not online. I'm guessing you have justified this decision to yourself and others for a long time and one or two paragraphs in this book are not going to overcome your hesitation; but let me try. There are likely three reasons that you are not online: time constraints (remember the twenty-minute rule, above), technical aptitude, or privacy concerns.

For those who are not tech-savvy, the idea of using any or all of these online tools may sound like torture. Good news: a lot of unemployed twenty-two-year-olds out there find social media as easy as breathing. Could you find one to help you? There are also great online classes, if you're open to learning.[34] (After all, you are asking others to learn what you have to teach; isn't it a good idea to have a learning mind of your own?)

If you are more inhibited by privacy concerns, there are fortunately lots of venues where you can play without revealing more than your name and maybe a few lines about your background or credentials. Comment on a blog, submit an online article, or retweet another thought leader. Start a private LinkedIn group or host or join a meetup. Speak on a panel, be a guest on a radio show. None of these requires much sharing of your personal information, and certainly not your credit card number.

Pledge Yourself in Service to Others

What's the biggest reason we hold back from putting ourselves on S.H.O.U.T.? Very often it is fear of exposure. What if we make a mistake, say the wrong thing, stumble, don't do it right? What if our ideas are judged harshly or others say, "Who do they think they are?"

As I began writing this book, I faced a few of my own demons. It took me a few weeks to put pen to paper as I dealt with my inner (very negative) voices. Speaking with other thought leaders, I've learned that we all worry about what others might think about us. Instead we need to remember to be in service to our audience and consider the importance of the *What If?* future we are working to bring about.

If fear of exposure holds you back try this:

- Focus on delivering real value.
- Identify quantitative and qualitative measures that will provide you the positive feedback that will keep you on track. (See Chapter Seven for more on this.)
- Look back at Chapter Four and identify some support techniques you can use. It might be time to activate your personal board of directors.

Overcome Their Objections

Katie Orenstein, creator of the OpEd Project, began training people how to formulate their ideas into a compelling argument in 2008.[35] Today, in addition to public seminars that are hosted monthly across the United States, the organization leads year-long fellowship programs coast-to-coast at ten major universities, including Stanford, Yale, and the University of California, San Francisco.

During her training programs, Orenstein asks every participant how often they change their minds when they hear a new argument or point of view. The consensus of this informal research is that most people rarely alter their viewpoint on something very important to them (almost always less than 10 percent of the time), even in light of new information presented compellingly—a disheartening statistic. But even more importantly, she's learned that "people will almost never change their mind if their original point of view is not respected or they do not sense empathy from the person who is introducing them to a new idea."[36] Perhaps that's why one-sided news broadcasts so rarely have an impact, except on those who already agree with the point of view of the broadcaster.

The OpEd Project training provides each participant time to argue their point of view but also to acknowledge and then try to overcome the objections that will arise when others hear that point of view. Not only does this exercise strengthen participants' arguments; it also toughens them and readies them for the real world, where not everyone will agree with them. It also teaches listening skills—a key element of understanding another's viewpoint.

If you can't attend an OpEd Project seminar, I recommend you create your own laboratory where you can experiment with and ready your arguments and learn to meet and respond to the disbelief or scrutiny of others. Think of it as debate prep, though it is just as important whether you will share your ideas through writing or speaking.

- Can you identify the counterarguments to what you believe?
- What proof points can you offer to counter others' objections?
- Who can help you practice "staying cool under fire" and prepare you to address others' objections with respect and empathy?

Commit to Spreading Happiness

Did you know that you can spread happiness? It's true. As Stanford Graduate School of Business professor Jennifer Aaker, one of the world's experts on happiness, tells us in her book *The Dragonfly Effect*, the "phenomenon whereby emotions you feel infect others is called *emotional contagion*."

She cites research showing that "People who are happy (or become happy) significantly boost the chances that their friends will become happy; and the power of happiness can span up to two more degrees of separation." "Further," she continues, "these contagious effects have a lasting impact. One individual's happiness can affect another's for as much as a year."[37]

Don't underestimate the value you can have for others when you share what you're up to and the successes you've had to date. Many people are ready to cheer you on and champion your wins. Your good news (and big ideas) can make others happy, and that happiness spreads. And we all need more happiness, don't we?

UNDERSTAND POTENTIAL PITFALLS

A lot of rewards can be had when you put yourself on S.H.O.U.T., even unexpected ones like spreading happiness. There are also potential pitfalls to avoid, including straying from principles of transparency; going outside your pond; trying to please everyone; becoming too predictable; or not matching your content to the level of your audience's expertise.

Transparency Counts

In the "Getting Started" chapter, we spoke about the importance of practicing journalistic principles—thoroughness, accuracy, fairness, independence, and transparency. As a thought leader, not following even one of these rules can lead you to enormous pitfalls. Identify and verify your sources. When you make a mistake, say so.

If you are propagating others' ideas, that's great; just be sure you clarify what's yours and what's theirs. Giving others credit is not only the right thing to do; it can also be an act of generosity and humility that will help you connect with audiences. It shows that you are constantly learning.

Stick to Your Pond

The good news is that if you've already taken the earlier steps in this book, you know which pond is yours. Now can I invite you to do your best to stick to it? I'm not suggesting you shouldn't venture out of your niche on occasion. Feel free to venture into an adjacent pond if you can add value there. But really, honestly, truly ... let me be the one to break it to you. *No one cares what you had for lunch.* Nor is it likely that they care what you think about Estonia's energy policy if your pond is industrial design.

On a more positive note, there is a lot to say in your pond, isn't there? You wouldn't have chosen it if you didn't think something important still needed to be said (and done) to create your *What If?* future. So please, say that instead. Your fans will love you for it.

Focus on Your 1,000 True Fans

And speaking of fans, it's probably good to remember that you can't please all the people all the time. This is a mantra I have to keep repeating to myself. Tim Ferris, author of the *4-Hour Work Week*, advises, "If you have 1,000 true fans who are perfectly curated [self-selected], by virtue of your material, you don't need to do marketing."[38] If you write and speak for the people who care about (and even love) what you have to say, you are much more likely to create evangelists for your ideas than if you spend *any* time worrying about those who don't.

Overcome the Al Gore Challenge

As the go-to person in your niche, every day you face what I call the "Al Gore challenge"—the danger of predictability. For years and years, Al Gore traveled from town to town sharing his message about the consequences of global warming. His standard talk was compelling, complete with a giant forklift that he rode in to make his point about the rising temperatures in our oceans, and with haunting pictures about the impending apocalypse. If you went to see him, you always knew what to expect. He had a book, a website, videos, and so on. He had a clear message and he stuck to it. Three-quarters of me would tell you that, as a result, he is the poster boy for great thought leadership. But one-quarter of me also thinks there is another lesson here.

There is a delicate balance between being reliable and being *boring*. Give yourself permission (and time) to renew, update, rethink, and reframe on a regular basis. To do that, you need to regularly assess the trends, incorporate the news of the day, and dig deeply into your well of expertise to constantly give your best ideas and lessons learned to your audience. Thought leadership isn't about being comfortable; it is about always ensuring you are the very best spokesperson you can be for the efforts you have under way.

Relevance Resonates

The content with the highest relevance—the most timely and on point with the audience—always wins. During the thirty-four-minute 2013 Super Bowl power outage, Orco tweeted a clever ad with the caption, "Power out? No problem. You can still dunk in the dark." This Twitter "ad" was retweeted over ten thousand times within the first hour. Why? It was relevant in the moment.[39]

As you create content—for a speech, podcast, video, or tweet—remember Nancy Duarte's advice and think through what you'd like your audience to think, do, or feel differently as a result of what you're saying or sharing. Are you talking about something relevant to them and their challenges? Are you adding value? Is what you have to say clever or compelling or timely?

If your audience is a lot of newbies, put yourself back in your beginner's shoes and think about what you wish you'd known when you were first starting out. If you're speaking more to your peers, think about the type of conversation you'd be having at a mastermind table (see Chapter Four).

Either way, sharing best practices, lessons learned, and new discoveries will never go out of style. Remember the metaphor of the Rider and the Elephant from Chapter Five? We all need to have a path forward, and many would be happy to take yours without having to go through the blood, sweat, and tears you may have experienced along the way.

It's not about different content for every audience—it's about offering a different lens on the same content. Keep imagining that *What If?* future you are creating. What will others need to know to imagine it too? You are in this together; help them see how they can engage with you to realize that future.

Say We, Not I

One type of article that I tend to home in on when I'm reading a magazine is one that promises "10 Lessons" or "6 Tips." I am always looking to pick up one more useful strategy. Thus, the *Forbes* article "8 Public Speaking Lessons from 57 Inaugural Speeches: The Good, The Bad, and the Ugly," by Margaret M. Perlis, caught my eye.[40] Perlis's lessons include the standard public speaking tips—"keep it concise," "know your audience," and so on. But she also includes one about the importance of using the first-person plural: "we."

There are times when it is critical to say "we" instead of "I." Perlis's example is the inaugural address of Theodore Roosevelt in 1905. Roosevelt's goal at that time was "to [bring] the American people into his huddle ... empowered as team members ... to work with him and each other to take responsibility for the greater good of the country."[41] He wanted to create the "we" in "team."

Early in my career as CEO of the Forum for Women Entrepreneurs, I was invited to speak at the board meeting for our new chapter in Seattle. This was my first chance to present to the group there, and I prepared an overview of our Bay Area efforts, our expansion plans, and much more. I probably spoke for twenty to thirty minutes (breaking Perlis's first rule). There were some nodding heads and smiles, but there were also some not-so-friendly faces at that table.

At the end of the talk, the board chair, Trish Zuccotti, then a director at Deloitte & Touche, took me aside and gave me a little piece of advice. "You did a great job," she told me. "But next time, you might say 'we' instead of 'I' to rally the troops." Lesson learned.

Which brings me to the *T* in S.H.O.U.T.: the importance of finding ways to coalesce individuals into a community.

TRANSFORM INDIVIDUALS INTO A COMMUNITY

If your goal is to broaden your impact beyond your organization, think about how to transform the individuals you've been meeting with one-on-one into a community around your cause. How can you S.H.O.U.T. in a way that scales your impact and builds individual fans into followers—those who identify themselves as part of a tribe? Show them how to engage with you and your ideas, and let them contribute their own knowledge and gifts.

Show Them How to Engage

When people read your blog, visit your website, find you on social media, or attend your talks, do they know how to spread the word or get involved in what you're up to? Close each interaction with a few engagement strategies—ways people can take action today. You will be far more likely to build a tribe if you do.

You could invite people to join your email list or attend an upcoming event. At the close of any blog post, encourage readers to submit a comment or forward the post to members of their network. Encourage visitors to your website or social media page to ask you a question, share, or retweet your content. Create options for engagement—a contest, a petition, an online class. And then make it easy for your visitors to subscribe to your email list, follow your blog, and recommend your content to their friends and colleagues, by adding all the necessary links.

Give something in return to those who sign up for your list or link to you. What could you give to your followers that would add value for them: top ten tips, forty great ideas, or an action list of ways to make a difference? Create free but high-value resource lists, as well as a white paper that shares your ideas more fully.

Let Them Contribute

How do you keep people coming back for more? You might think that people like to engage with you because you have all the answers. But the opposite is actually true.

To really transform a fan into a follower, you must let them contribute.

Why? It turns out, people actually value something far more when they had a hand in creating it. Researchers call this the "Ikea Effect," after the unexpected finding that people who put together their own Ikea desk tend to value it more than a desk they purchased ready-made.[42] In other words, the very act of cocreating a finished product allows people to find that it has value.

Move as quickly as possible from being the "sage from the stage"—where you are the one with all of the information and they are there to listen—to having a genuine conversation. Open the door to a dialogue between you and your followers, and among your followers as well. This is often a shift in mind-set as much as it is a modification of your natural modus operandi. Thought leaders are by nature subject-matter experts, and they like to educate.

But you are also there to learn.

The thought leaders I have seen who can actively engage with people and show that they are open to new ideas are the ones who continue to grow their followership. Thought leadership is a constant learning exercise.

Here are a few examples of what community engagement might look like:

- When you give a talk, ask the audience for their questions up front and then speak to your audience's interests rather than what you believe they need to know. If that isn't possible, allow for an open Q&A session and encourage members of the audience to answer each other's questions.
- Create a Facebook fan page and invite visitors to provide each other advice and solve each other's problems. Ask everyone to share best practices and resources.
- Create a Google+ event and invite three other subject-matter experts to co-lead the conversation with you, sharing their thoughts and ideas equally with yours.
- Create a LinkedIn group but share the moderation of the group's activities so others feel an equal commitment to build continued engagement.
- When you tweet, be sure to also retweet other thought leaders' great ideas rather than think of them as the "competition." Encourage your followers to not only focus attention on their own successes but also share how they are working together.

There are hundreds of ways in which to build an engaged community—we'll talk more about this in the next chapter. In the meantime, study some of the top thought leaders in your niche. How do they act online or in person? What will you emulate, and what should you be sure to avoid?

START WITH THE BASICS

To put yourself on S.H.O.U.T. can feel overwhelming. I don't want to leave this chapter without stating the basics. What should you do today to be discoverable? If you only do three things:

1. Collect cards and contact information from people that you meet and create an email list (I like Constant Contact[43]).

2. Create a top-notch LinkedIn profile and connect online with those you meet.
3. Write about your ideas and submit them to a well-trafficked blog.

That's it, really.

Why would I start with these? With a LinkedIn profile, others can find you. With an email list, you can connect with those who share your interests. And when you write in a well-trafficked forum, others will learn about your ideas; further, journalists will begin to rely on you as a source for content.

Those are the basics. Even if you just start there, you will begin to have an impact.

Of course, I really hope you won't stop there. When you're ready to go to the next level, look below at "More Food for Thought" for more ideas and resources, or turn to the next chapter where we'll discuss how to audit, accelerate, and amplify your activities.

PUT YOURSELF ON S.H.O.U.T.: A QUICK REVIEW

In this step of the thought leadership journey, successful thought leaders

- Test their ideas, study others' successes, and find small venues where they can learn what resonates
- Develop a quality personal brand and unique point of view, which they remain true to no matter what
- Learn to tell great stories, including their own and those of their "customers"
- Identify pictures, data, arguments, and proof points that help tell their story and overcome objections to their ideas
- Develop a clear set of keywords or phrases they can call their own

- Practice strategic ubiquity, identifying a few platforms where they can be accessible to their audience and maintain an active presence
- Overcome their own objections to putting themselves on S.H.O.U.T. by pledging themselves in the service of others and committing to spreading happiness
- Adhere to standard journalistic principles and stay focused on the needs of others
- Provide opportunities for their followers to engage, contribute, and share their stories with one another
- Start with the basics—ensure they are discoverable, connect with their community, and share their ideas widely

MORE FOOD FOR THOUGHT

Venues and Selection Criteria

Whether you are starting out or have been at this a while, putting yourself on S.H.O.U.T. will increase your impact and expand your influence, first internally within your organization, then with your peers in your industry, and then across industries. You'll grow your followership first locally, and then regionally, then to other states and even neighboring countries, until you have a global reach. Here are additional ideas for how to make this transition, and more things to consider as you select what to do first.

S.H.O.U.T. Venues for Those New to Thought Leadership

In your organization: Write for your organization's newsletter; host a brown-bag lunch; compose or cowrite a white paper; start an internal wiki or create a short video about your team's activities; submit a blog post to the company blog; send a monthly email to interested employees; create a set of downloadable talking points and slides for others so they can host a five-minute meeting for their team that provides an overview of your activities.

In your industry: Speak on a panel for an industry event; join the organizing committee for an industry conference; serve on a selection committee for an industry award; write an article for an industry magazine or website; start a blog or submit a guest blog post to a popular site; convene a group of people who share your expertise.

In your community: Be a guest speaker at a local event or on a local radio show; contact a journalist to get press for your activities; write an op-ed; join a task force; convene or join a Meetup; write an article for the neighborhood newspaper.

S.H.O.U.T. Venues for Experts

In your organization: Offer to serve as the company spokesperson with the press; identify a well-known subject-matter expert and cowrite a white paper with them; develop a series of how-to videos or podcasts and get agreement to host them on the company's website; offer to take over management of the company blog; submit information about your team's activities to the company's annual report or an awards committee; ask to present your successes at the annual board meeting; convene or serve on a cross-organization task force; self-publish or publish a book.

In your industry: Offer to put together a panel of experts for an industry event; seek an invitation to keynote a conference; found or lead an industry association; apply for an industry award; start a new industry award and develop your own criteria and judges panel; secure a standing column in a well-respected magazine or website; create or provide leadership for an industry consortium; join an advisory, regulatory, or legislative committee; testify before Congress; join the board of a prestigious foundation; syndicate your content to an industry magazine; join the board or advisory board of a start-up; cocreate a research report with a well-respected academic researcher; self-publish or publish a book.

In your community: Keynote or emcee an important community event; join the chamber of commerce; chair a local fundraiser; apply for a prestigious award; chair a task force; run for office; create a new event that serves a needy neighborhood or constituency; write a regular column for or syndicate your content to a local newspaper; get an invitation to be interviewed on the radio during drive time; self-publish or publish a book.

(continued)

Selection Criteria: So Many Opportunities, so Little Time

As you begin to get better known, you will receive more and more opportunities to put yourself on S.H.O.U.T. Below are some selection criteria to consider as you narrow your choices. Prioritize these for yourself and use them as your funnel.

- Will I connect with people I need to know or want to know?
- Will I gain access to others who could make needed introductions or could serve as role models, sponsors, advisors, employees, or mentors?
- Will I reach my intended audience or a group of people that has influence with those in my target audience?
- Will I have the opportunity to test and hone my ideas?
- Will I be able to change minds, behaviors, or actions?
- Will I move forward an agenda I care deeply about?
- Will there be any remuneration or a donation to my favorite cause?
- Do I have something unique or important to say that needs to be heard?
- Will I gain needed skills, knowledge, experiences, perspectives, or know-how?
- Will I have a seat at the table where important decisions are being made?
- Will I have the chance to impress others with my expertise and ideas?
- Will I benefit from seeing big problems (in my industry or area of expertise) in new ways?
- Will the downside risk be low or manageable?
- Do I understand the time commitment and can I meet it?

CHAPTER 7

INCITE (R)EVOLUTION

In the last two chapters, we focused on how to distill your knowledge and experiences into best practices or into a methodology, and how to S.H.O.U.T. about your activities to the world. Now it's time to focus on what it takes to build true momentum for your efforts—momentum that causes your *What If?* future to become a here-today reality.

This involves accelerating the pace at which people learn about, adopt, and help you scale your efforts—which in turn means continuing our conversation about how to engage people to move from the sidelines and get engaged on the playing field. Here we'll discuss how to audit, accelerate, and amplify your voice, your influence, and your impact, and how to make certain that you don't burn out along the way.

AUDIT YOUR IMPACT

Imagine that you could see a map of the world and all across it are blinking lights representing people who know about you, have heard about your ideas, or have adopted new ways of thinking or behaving as a result of your ideas. What if, even as you watched, you could observe more and more lights blink on and the landscape illuminate before your eyes?

As each of your fans spreads the word about your ideas, you would see more lights blink on, radiating out from each of them. As fans became more knowledgeable, engaged, and on fire to share what they know, they would build on what you've accomplished. The lights would spread more quickly. Over time, rather than lots of little lights scattered here and there, you would soon see campfires glowing, then bonfires blazing, and soon the whole world would be alight.

That would be amazing, wouldn't it? We'd all like to imagine the world alight with our ideas!

Since we don't actually have a map that lights up as our ideas spread, we have to find other ways to analyze our impact. We do this by auditing the online and offline signals that show the evolutionary and revolutionary transformations under way.

Auditing your activities—tracking your engagement quantitatively and qualitatively—will help you ensure that you stay connected with your audience and spread your ideas from a few lights to campfires spanning the horizon. Auditing will also give you a bird's-eye view of what others in your ecosystem are doing and talking about, which will not only help you stay current but allow you to work together with those already engaged to start wildfires of evolutionary and revolutionary change.

Auditing can take many forms. Some people simply collect business cards and build an email list, measuring its growth year by year. Others measure their engagement by the number of followers they have on social media. Some write content in a blog, a Wikipedia page, or the op-ed section of a major publication and watch as their ideas are linked to, quoted, and spark public discourse. Still others enjoy speaking and measure their impact by the size of their audience or how often they are invited to speak. Press coverage can also be tracked and tallied.

You'll likely find that as you "put yourself on S.H.O.U.T.," you will spark more and more new opportunities and venues to share your ideas and more and more followers to push your initiatives forward. As I began to speak about our efforts at the Forum for Women Entrepreneurs for small local conferences and online and offline events (this was before blogs, Facebook, and Twitter), those who learned about our efforts brought together friends and colleagues and replicated our activities in their communities. When I invited local newspaper journalists to our events, their coverage led me to opportunities to appear on radio and TV. These appearances led to a book deal, funding for our organization, and opportunities to join the national conversation about women's entrepreneurship.

As you build your own credibility through social media, blog mentions, and expert citations, you'll find your own influence growing, often exponentially. Soon you may find that it takes more than an email list to keep up with the spread of your ideas. Fortunately, there are a number of ways to audit and track your impact using online monitoring and alerts, influence mapping, and reputation management tools.

Online influence mapping tools measure three things: resonance, relevance, and reach. Ideas light up the world if they *resonate* with the audience. Ideas resonate if people find the message *relevant* and the messenger credible. They resonate if the message is clear and easy to understand and if it is received in the appropriate milieu (platform, context, timing). Once someone hears a message that excites them, they are likely to tell others. This extends your *reach*.

How do you know when your message is resonating—when people are talking about you or your ideas online? You can set up simple alerts for news stories, blogs, and social media mentions.

You can also track your online influence over time using influence mapping tools that score your ability to make a connection with your audience, and how their efforts help you scale your reach.

- Set up a Google alert (www.google.com/alerts) to monitor when your name (or your keywords) appears online.
- Set up a Social Mention alert (www.socialmention.com) to monitor when you (and other top influencers in your ecosystem) are mentioned in social media.
- Create RSS (which stands for Really Simple Syndication) alerts to monitor when your name appears in someone else's blog post, or to alert you when other top influencers are blogging. RSS alert tools (Technorati, Google Blog Search, and so on) all monitor different blogging platforms, or you can set up an RSS reader to monitor the blogs that are most likely to be talking about you or the subjects you care about.[1]
- Use Newsle (www.newsle.com) to stay informed when those in your network appear in the press. Newsle scans your personal contacts, LinkedIn connections, and other social contacts online and then sends you an email when any of them are in the news.
- Klout (www.klout.com) ranks your influence online with a Klout Score (1–100). The more engagement and action that you inspire with the content you create (likes, shares, retweets), the greater your influence and the higher your Klout Score.
- Brand Yourself (www.brandyourself.com) is an online reputation site that is focused on helping individuals improve their online brand. It's set up to be simple to use and do-it-yourself—giving you control over your searches.[2]

This is actually only the beginning of the online tools. If you're ready to go to the next level, head to "More Food for Thought" at the end of the chapter, or visit the Thought Leadership Lab website.[3]

ACCELERATE YOUR INFLUENCE

Up until now, we've been exploring different "one-to-many" modes for sharing your ideas: writing, speaking, social media, video, or building a website. These are all great starting points. But real scale happens when you move from a one-to-many to a many-to-many model—where others are empowered to carry your ideas forward to their communities. Think back over some of the thought leaders we've talked about in the book. How did they accelerate their influence? And how did they measure whether they were having the intended impact?

As Zoe Dunning sought to overturn the "Don't Ask, Don't Tell" policy of the U.S. military, she spoke widely, gave frequent press interviews, and advocated her position before Congress. She started a nonprofit advocacy group and regularly connected with others who shared her convictions and had their own efforts under way.

When Mary Hughes aspired to increase the number of women running for national office, she partnered with the Center for American Women and Politics to create a national campaign; formed a partnership alliance with local nonprofits; hosted and spoke at events; and used social media. She also pursued a train the trainer model, creating a national faculty that could share the same messages with a much wider audience.

To share his expertise in web analytics and digital marketing, Avinash Kaushik started a blog, then wrote two books, and actively uses social media. He also gives paid speeches. He measures his impact by the number of followers on his blog and social media; the frequency of his fan emails; and the impact he can have with charitable donations using income from his books.

Van Ton-Quinlivan wants to broaden access to education, improve the way students are educated, and expand funding for education. She speaks nationally, uses social media sparingly, serves on national boards and commissions, gives regular press interviews, and partners widely to spread the word. She measures her outcomes

Name & Chapter	Engagement Strategies								How They Measured Impact
	Speaking	Social Media	Press and/or OpEds	Advocating Nationally	Partnerships	Hosted Events	Train the Trainers	Books	
Zoe Dunning, Chapter 4	X		X	X					Successful repeal of the "Don't Ask, Don't Tell" policy
Mary Hughes, Chapter 3	X	X	X		X	X	X (Faculty)		Number of women who attended events, ran for office, and won
Avinash Kaushik, Chapter 7	X	X						X	Followers on social media, fan emails, income/charitable donations
Van Ton-Quinlivan, Chapter 2	X		X	X	X	X			Number of companies and individuals adopting her ideas nationally; legislative changes

by the number of people adopting her ideas as well as the impact she can make on state and national legislation.

Speaking, social media, press and op-eds, national advocacy, partnerships, hosted events, training the trainers, books, blogs: which of these strategies will you adopt? And what other options can you identify for accelerating the adoption of your ideas and moving more quickly towards your *What If?* future? Here are some examples from others to inspire you to think more broadly.

Robin Chase

Transportation innovator Robin Chase is pursuing a big *What If?* future: How can we transform the world from an industrial economy to a collaborative economy? In addition to founding car-sharing company Zipcar, ride-sharing company GoLoco, and peer-to-peer car rental company Buzzcar, she measures her impact by her ability to influence government policies and the way big companies behave. To do that, she speaks widely at conferences and universities and participates on government commissions like the Intelligent Transportation Systems Program Advisory Committee, advising Congress on transportation issues, as well as the National Council on Innovation and Entrepreneurship for the secretary of commerce. She joins global conversations at places like the World Economic Forum and writes op-eds that gain widespread attention through venues like the *New York Times*. She guest blogs, is active on social media, hosts webinars where she shares her ideas, and is at work on a book to share her far-reaching views about the future of the collaborative economy.[4]

Jerry McNellis

Jerry McNellis developed the "Compression Planning" system, a "surprisingly easy-to-understand planning process that combines strategic thinking and decision-making and delivers amazing results in a short amount of time." Since 1978, he and his team have trained over fifteen thousand individuals in their system. Today their followers host national institutes across the United States and bring together their own communities to learn the Compression Planning methodology. McNellis continues to lead Compression Planning sessions at companies, nonprofits, and in the community college system; his method has revolutionized fundraising and strategic planning for many institutions.[5]

Katharine Briggs and Isabel Briggs Myers

The Myers-Briggs Type Indicator (MBTI) is administered over 1.5 million times annually to individuals, including the employees of most Fortune 500 companies. It was codified in 1923 by Katharine Briggs and her daughter Isabel Briggs Myers, who spread the word through articles and books before partnering with the Educational Testing Service to cement the MBTI as a standard. One of their followers started the Typology Laboratory at the University of Florida in 1970. In 1975, Myers established the Center for Applications of Psychology Type as an independent not-for-profit organization, and it hosted the first international conference of MBTI practitioners. Next they formed a membership organization and a foundation, put the assessment online, and began a certification program. Today the Myers and Briggs Foundation certifies thousands of MBTI practitioners worldwide. They also license international distributors who provide MBTI training, translations, and support materials. The MBTI Master Practitioner Referral Network connects all of the practitioners together.[6]

George Ward

In 1993, George Ward was hired by Cisco to expand the company's reach into the education market. He quickly learned that what was needed was training for educators in how to maintain Cisco networks in schools. His first classes, intended for high school teachers and staff, soon attracted savvy high school students as well. Ward went to Cisco's CEO and got his buy-in to start a high school training program. Within three years, the Cisco Networking Academy had expanded to sixty-four high schools in seven states. By 2012, there were over ten thousand academies in 165 countries and more than four million students had participated in the training.

Ward began by creating a forty-hour training program, which included a PowerPoint presentation and hands-on activities. He hired experts who knew how to create training for high school students, and then online curriculum experts to put the program on the Internet.[7] The program has grown to include case studies, simulations, interactive tools, educational games, online assessments, social media tools, and an online instructor community site that connects students and instructors around the world.[8]

Dennis Littky

Dennis Littky, a longtime educator and high school principal, has always had radical ideas about education. When he was approached by the commissioner of education of Rhode Island to start a new high school, Littky and his friend Elliott Washor set out to rethink education. Within four years, every one of the students who attended the Met School (as it was known) got accepted to college and their dropout rate was 2 percent instead of the local average of 46 percent. Five million dollars in funding from the Gates Foundation allowed them to create twelve more schools, and by 2012 they had sixty schools in five countries adopting their ideas.

Not one to rest on his laurels, in 2009 Littky went on to found a college program (College UnBound) based on the same tenets.[9] He has also founded and now leads Big Picture Learning, a nonprofit organization that encompasses all of his activities. The organization's advisors consult with other educators, families, and communities, sharing proven programs of study in order to help them start their own schools. As these advisors learn from the educators' experiences, they continuously improve the design of their high school and college programs. Littky and his team also offer training for principals and teachers, chair symposiums on career and technical education, and work to influence public policy.[10]

Michelle May

Dr. Michelle May was a practicing physician who had her own secret struggle with food and body image. She began teaching mindful-eating workshops "on the side" while she had a full-time medical practice. Fourteen years later, she has "retired" from medicine and her "Am I Hungry" Mindful Eating Workshops are now available through corporate wellness programs, medical offices, hospitals, fitness centers, insurance companies, and community programs. She has appeared on radio and TV and has spoken before tens of thousands as a certified speaking professional (CSP).

What began as an eight-week, in-person workshop and workbook offered to her patients, May turned into books, keynotes, and a train-the-trainer and licensing program. She initially trained Am I Hungry facilitators through teleseminars and webinars, but now the training is available online through a self-paced course that attracts licensees from around the world. Continuing education (CE) credits for the program broaden its reach for nurses, registered dieticians, and psychologists who are required to complete a certain number of CE credits annually. She has also created a five-day intensive retreat that builds community and reinforces behavior change, and she has hired someone to help her operationalize her corporate workshops.

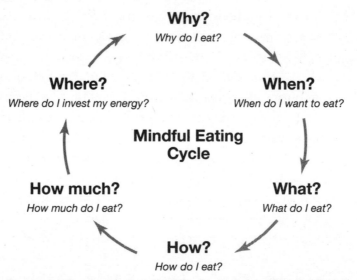

Reprinted with permission from *Eat What You Love, Love What You Eat* by Michelle May, M.D., CSP

To continue to spread the word about the Am I Hungry mindful-eating concepts, May is a frequent guest speaker at community wellness events and medical conferences. She has been an invited guest expert on radio and TV news programs and health and wellness shows, including the Discovery Health Channel and Dr. Oz. She blogs, writes articles, and has an active social media program. Her book *Eat What You Love, Love What You Eat* was selected as the basis for the American Academy of Family Physician's national wellness campaign, "Americans in Motion."[11]

As you can see, when you choose to scale your activities, you have many different options. You can join existing conversations in your ecosystem or start your own; you can spread your ideas through training, consulting, speaking, writing, or advising. You can join a board, committee, or commission. You can work for legislative or regulatory change or build academies or institutes that will carry on your work. You can convene conferences or build an online community of trainers and distributors.[12] The paths you could take to accelerate your impact are as wide and varied as you could wish. But please don't be daunted. These examples are meant to spark your ideas, not overwhelm you. Like Robin, Jerry, Katharine, Isabel, George, Dennis, and Michelle, you will start where you are today and build incrementally. It all starts with small steps.

Small Steps, Big Change

As Professor Jennifer Aaker of Stanford Business School has learned from her extensive research on change, "Sometimes people think that creating big change means taking big steps towards that big change." But what her research has shown is that "small acts are oftentimes more effective." She recommends that you set "micro-goals" and work to achieve those tiny little goals rather than setting enormous goals that will seem too daunting and prevent you from moving forward.

As we engage others, her research shows that we must also set micro-goals for them—create a small, single, focused goal that is easy to see and achieve. Three things are required. First, to grab people's attention, you should design goals that are unusual or unexpected. Secondly, you should create highly engaging actions for them to take. This will entice them to notice—to "lean in and look." Finally, you must create "acts that are actionable." These are clear paths for people to follow so that they will become a part of what you have under way.[13] (For more detailed advice, I highly recommend Aaker's book *The Dragonfly Effect*.[14])

When you grab people's attention, you will find that your ideas are heard. But if you can also get people to act, you will accelerate your impact—sparking others to add their actions to yours to together create much broader transformation. To then fan these sparks into bonfires, you will need to gather these change-makers into a community and empower them to carry your ideas forward, which includes building their own communities to spread new ideas and innovations as far and wide as possible.

AMPLIFY YOUR VOICE

One of the things I learned in my years as an executive at Motorola was that if you don't train the next generation of leaders to follow in your footsteps, you'll never get promoted. The same thinking applies to any endeavor you have underway. As top business coach Kate Purmal advises her start-up clients, "Don't build a business without an exit strategy." She works with them "to anticipate how they need to scale their infrastructure so their business can operate without them."[15]

Lest you think that I'm off on some tangent here, the fact is that thought leaders could learn a lot from Purmal's advice. If you develop YouTube videos, webinars, or online courses, or if you create workbooks, training materials, or certification programs, you are making your work accessible to much wider audiences and communities. These projects may also bring in money to sustain your efforts. The materials you develop to document your thinking and guiding principles become the infrastructure your followers can build upon to spread your ideas more widely—without you.

Empowering followers is a three-step process: you do something (what we covered in Chapters One through Four); you teach others to do something (Chapters Five and Six); and then they learn to do it without you (this chapter). The guiding principle for this stage is to realize that your success is reflected in your followers' excellence. The more you can empower them as individuals and as a community, the better. In addition to codifying your ideas, build a group of followers that can sustain those ideas and is itself sustained for years to come. That is what it takes to leave a meaningful legacy.

Create a Follower Community

What if you had a fan club? I am revealing my age here, but I remember watching Annette Funicello on the *Mickey Mouse Club* show when I was little, and thinking, *I want to be a Mouseketeer*. There was something very compelling about being part of a group of fans like that. Since then, we've seen Jimmy Buffet and his more than two hundred chapters of Parrot Heads, and Lady Gaga and her more than twenty million Little Monsters. It might feel a little presumptuous right now to think that your community might grow as large as either of theirs, but that doesn't mean you can't start thinking of your friends, fans, and followers as part of a community.

The benefit of creating a followership is that the members of a network can begin to support and learn from one another. To move from individual fans to a mutually supportive community: create a membership designation, develop community norms, gather the community together, find ways to honor their participation, designate the next generation who will carry the community forward, and connect the community to the larger ecosystem.

Create a Membership Designation   Not every community lends itself to a membership model, but it is perhaps the easiest way to create a community. When we first started the Forum for Women Entrepreneurs (FWE), we had a loose designation of membership: everyone was welcome and there was no membership fee. But over time we realized that to move our agenda forward—accelerating the amount of venture financing going to women entrepreneurs—we should be more selective. We created a membership application and charged a modest fee. This allowed us to focus our attention on those most likely to benefit from our efforts. It also created a community among FWE members that encouraged them to support one another.

Membership fees per se are not required. Dennis Littky's community is made up of the leaders of the schools he has founded as well as those who have adopted his ideas to build their own. Michelle May's followers include people who have read her books and adopted her ideas as well as those who are trained and licensed to spread the Am I Hungry model more widely. Jerry McNellis has an online forum for everyone who has ever gone through the Compression Planning training, and his team regularly sends them new ideas and updates.

Develop Community Norms   At FWE, our guiding principle, right from the beginning, was that no member should come to an event with their hand out, expecting others to serve them. If you wanted to receive, you needed to start by giving—your expertise, connections, ideas, even your volunteer time—to ensure that everyone was more successful. Establishing norms for how your community will behave, and then reiterating and modeling those behaviors, will serve you well in creating both an insider status and a self-sustaining entity.

Gather the Community Together   Michelle May hosts five-day retreats for renewal and learning; Dennis Littky hosts an annual national conference for idea-sharing and to rally and galvanize followers; and the MBTI Master Practitioners attend annual global events to learn from experts and share best practices and business tips. What might a gathering of your followers look like? You might choose to host online or offline events, encourage others to host events, or have local, national, or international gatherings.

Sheryl Sandberg, the COO of Facebook, created widespread adoption for the ideas in her book *Lean In* when she partnered with Gina Bianchini, CEO of Mightybell, and Stanford University.[16] By using Mightybell technology, Sandberg encouraged her followers to gather with friends and colleagues to create "Lean In" circles, then pushed regular updates and educational content developed by Stanford professors to members of these circles to engage and empower them to "lean in" to their careers.[17]

Honor Community Members   Everyone loves to win an award. How can you recognize those who exemplify your values or have made an outsize contribution? Award ceremonies are also great for bringing people together in celebration. At FWE, we hosted an annual awards dinner that became our best fundraiser and my favorite night of the year. Hosted at a local hotel, this evening event brought the whole FWE ecosystem together to celebrate and gave me a chance to share a mini "State of the Union" address with the many members and potential members in the audience. It became a great networking and recruiting venue.

Designate the Next Generation   While this may not be possible, many thought leaders choose to designate the next generation who will continue to amplify their work. Michelle May certifies those who have completed her training programs so that they have the right to use her brand and materials within their organizations. George Ward provides his academy graduates with a variety of different certifications, and the MBTI community not only certifies practitioners but also licenses distributors who can train and certify others around the world.

Connect Your Community to the Broader Ecosystem
There are many others who care about what your community cares about. Encourage your followers to join the conversation with others who are part of the wider ecosystem. Together you will have

a greater chance to move forward and make a difference on a broad scale. You will also learn from and be able to adopt ideas from those in other regions who are tackling similar challenges. If there are no events connecting the broader ecosystem, perhaps you should host one.

TAKE CARE OF YOURSELF

As you know, evolutionary and revolutionary transformation doesn't happen overnight. Indeed, change making can be very exhausting (and even frustrating) work; even with a network of followers to help us amplify and accelerate our efforts, improving the status quo and engaging others to get on board can begin to feel like a herculean effort. I don't want to leave this chapter or end this book without a word about sustainability strategies—for you personally and in order to guarantee the ongoing adoption and expansion of your ideas.

A word of caution from one change agent to another: You will get tired. If you don't pace yourself, you will burn out. I know—because I did.

By April 2001, FWE had grown to seven offices, 1,200 members, and a staff of ten. We had been riding high as the whirlwind of the dot-com frenzy led to more and more women starting companies, joining the organization, and getting funding. But it all came to a crashing halt as the dot-com bubble became the dot-com bust virtually overnight. Not only was entrepreneurship no longer cool; the IPO market was no longer hot and the money to support our national efforts dried up overnight.

I lay awake night after night, the same endless calculations playing over and over in my head. First I totaled up how much money I expected to bring in before month's end to fund our organization, and then I subtracted out every expense I needed to pay to keep the organization afloat. The final calculated total was always so close to zero that I'd panic and begin again. Over and over it went as I wondered, *What if this check doesn't arrive?*

or *What if I've forgotten some bill that still needs to be paid?* It wasn't rational, yet I couldn't seem to stop going over the calculations until, eventually, the panicked feeling would subside and after another hour or so of tossing and turning, I would finally fall asleep, exhausted.

I learned something about myself through that experience: I don't reach out instinctively to get help. I don't like to admit problems. Looking back, I realize I had some sort of odd belief that this major economic downturn that affected the entire global economy was somehow my doing and I needed to fix it all by myself. Right!

Sadly, I was not alone in this mistaken reality. Although I was running the Forum for *Women* Entrepreneurs, calls that I received during this period were almost all from male entrepreneurs across Silicon Valley and the United States, asking for my advice and counsel and connections to help them save their companies. They were eagerly reaching out to anyone who could make an introduction for them to a banker or lawyer or accountant who had the inside scoop on what it took to survive.

Where were the women entrepreneurs? They were hiding under their beds. OK, I'm exaggerating slightly, but I did notice a sense among the women around me that this was an individual problem to be solved rather than a global phenomenon that no one individual should try to survive alone.

Fortunately, my organization did survive. We laid off staff, we cut programs and started new ones targeted to the new reality, and we found new funding sources. And I learned that it was unrealistic of me to think that I could solve all of our organization's problems all by myself. Hiding under my bed was *not* a strategy. What did work was reaching out to others—my board, advisory board, sponsors, and supporters—and letting them in on what we were facing. With their help, and their checks, we pulled through, together.

The organization celebrated its twentieth anniversary in 2013 with a new name, Watermark, and a broader mission. Today I serve on the emeritus board and celebrate as new leaders make their mark and carry on my legacy. Every time I attend an event or see our members in the news, I am honored that others continue my work to bring women more access to the C-suite, boardroom, and investment community. I know that a long road still lies ahead to attain the *What If?* future that we originally envisioned. Despite the setbacks and obstacles along the way, I am very proud of all we have already achieved.

No matter how you envision your own *What If?* future, you will face obstacles along the way. I can almost guarantee it. But take a lesson from me and don't isolate yourself at those times. Don't blame yourself or believe you have failed. Instead reach out to your allies and champions, to your friends, fans, and followers: seek their support, advice, and counsel and let them share your challenges.

As I was interviewing the thought leaders whom I included in this book, I asked some of them what keeps them going. Michelle May told me, "I would say, first of all, that not everyone is suited for this kind of work. I have a tremendous amount of energy, a huge amount of passion. I think a lot of us do who do this type of work—we find the meaning comes from a personal passion. And that is a huge driver for me—the desire to change the world and transform how the world thinks about eating and physical activity. You have to have that passion yourself."

She also assured me that she "practices what she preaches"—applying the mindfulness concepts of the Am I Hungry programs, "not just to eating but to how I live my life." She has also found that "mindful eating has become a pathway for people to live more mindfully and therefore more vibrantly. The work has become much bigger than what it originally started out to be."[18] That larger conversation motivates and energizes her to continue.

Ellen Leanse, executive VP of Eastwick Communications, whose work includes advising CEOs and executives on their thought leadership strategy, recommends to her clients that they set initial goals that are realistic and practicable, then revisit them quarterly. She invites them to answer four questions:

- What is success—what is the named destination that you identify as success?
- How will you know when you've reached that destination?
- What checkpoints or metrics will give you an early indication that you are on—or off—track so that you can course-correct?
- How will you measure to prove you've reached your success goal?

We all measure success differently. For some, it's quantitative measures, like the number of followers on Twitter, attendees in an audience, or how many times you are followed or quoted or referenced. For others, it might be more qualitative: Are you receiving invitations to ever higher-impact events, more-prestigious boards, or more-visible speaking venues? It could be seeing the impact that your efforts are having on others: Are people starting programs, initiatives, or events where they discuss or replicate your ideas? Are people changing their minds, behaviors, and attitudes as a result of what you recommend? Leanse advises that you also "check in with a business partner, a loved one, a coach or a best friend" who can help you judge how you're doing.[19]

As you see your own impact and influence grow, and you join the broader global conversations about what you care about, you'll find your own reasons to stay energized. But when you hit a speed bump, rather than putting your head down and focusing on what is just ahead of you or isolating yourself in your own room (or under your bed), try another path.

Seek support. Rest and rejuvenate. Remember to connect. And turn over the baton to others and let them carry it for a while.

Together, you'll be far more likely to stay the course and achieve the finish line.

Now that you have found your niche, built your inner and outer circle of supporters, codified your lessons learned, made yourself discoverable, and amplified your ideas through a community of followers, you have the platform, credibility, and influence to bring about important transformations in the arenas you care about. You will also have more opportunities to join and lead conversations that matter and bring about sustainable evolutionary and even revolutionary change. Enjoy the journey.

INCITE (R)EVOLUTION: A QUICK REVIEW

In this step of the thought leadership journey, successful thought leaders

- Measure their reach, resonance, and relevance online and off
- Use whatever technology they are comfortable with to ensure they measure and track their share of voice over time
- Create not only friends, fans, and followers but a follower community—word-of-mouth ambassadors who can learn from, share ideas with, and support one another
- Identify ways to create connections, online or off, among their followers
- Train and certify others to replicate their activities through a documented curriculum, training institute, certification program, licensees, or distributors
- Reach out to others to find support, advice, and counsel in order to prevent burnout
- Determine the success they are working towards, set qualitative and quantitative goals to measure their progress, and find someone to help them stay on track

MORE FOOD FOR THOUGHT

Additional Audit Tools

For those who love technology, or know how to hire people who do, it's an exciting time to be involved in the world of thought leadership because so many tools are available to measure and track your impact, influence, and share of voice. Are you one of the top thought leaders in your niche; are others adopting your ideas; are your ideas gaining traction, or not? Even a few years ago, to find the answers to these questions meant hiring a PR agency or a clipping service to create a scrapbook of your press clippings. Today the online influence mapping tools are not only very good; they continue to evolve rapidly.

Measure Your Share of Voice

Even a blogging tool like WordPress.com, an email list manager like Constant Contact, or a standard Twitter analyzer like Twitalyzer will let you track and monitor your influence to your heart's content. It is quite easy to determine which of your posts are forwarded or commented on by your community. (Of course, the downside is that the amount of detailed information that is available from even one of these tools can overwhelm you.)

If you're ready to take it to the next level, there is Traackr and their influencer discovery and mapping tool, A-List Platform.[20] Traackr is designed to be used by journalists looking for sources, conference organizers looking for speakers, and others who are trying to find people like you—influencers and thought leaders in a particular niche. When you understand what they are measuring—your topics and keywords, your site traffic and followers, your social conversations and

(continued)

associated social responses (shares, mentions, comments, and so on)—you can guarantee that you are focused only on what matters to raise your ranking.

If you don't have the budget to hire an agency or a consultant to monitor your influence online, there are lots of inexpensive tools for doing this yourself. I've already mentioned Klout and BrandYourself. Here are a few others, and you'll find a full list on our website at www.thoughtleadershiplab.com.

- Google's "What Do You Love" (www.wdyl.com) allows you to search for keywords across twenty different Google services so you can identify those that are trending and select those you will align to.
- Followerwonk (www.followerwonk.com) creates "super-actionable visualizations to compare your social graph to others."
- Mention (www.Mention.net) lets you create alerts so you know when you've been mentioned online; it even ranks the influence and authority of the source of that mention.
- Twylah (www.twylah.com) is an easy way to find trending people and topics. It also helps you turn your tweets into a website and create widgets out of your tweets.

Select one or a few of these tools to track those things that are important to you. Experiment to see which provides you with the best data for the least amount of effort. Once you've set up the system, it should mostly take care of itself. You can then set a monthly or quarterly reminder on your calendar to monitor the results and make adjustments accordingly.

If you find that some of your blog posts, tweets, or talks are generating a lot of conversation, focus more in those areas. If certain topics are trending online, align your efforts to those trends. These tools will also help you find other prominent and influential thought leaders to learn from and affiliate with as you broaden your connections and increase your influence and impact within your ecosystem.

CONCLUSION

*"We delight in the beauty of the butterfly, but
rarely admit the changes it has gone through to
achieve that beauty."*[1]

When I first began writing this book, I envisioned my own *What If?* future. What if there were more empowered people engaged with solving the world's biggest problems? What if they could share their ideas, codify their lessons learned, and gain widespread adoption for their innovative solutions? What if they knew how to build a community of followers eager to join them in implementing those solutions—and who would then carry on their work long after they were gone? Wouldn't the world be a better place?

I hope I have given you the tools and the resources to be one of those people. In fact, I hope you are well on your way.

I am confident you will find delight in your own metamorphosis from leader to thought leader and I invite you to celebrate your achievements and the transformation of the entire community you've inspired to make a difference in the world.

Whatever problem you are solving, whatever community you are serving, whatever idea you are propagating, I encourage you to utilize the seven-step thought leadership process, not once but over and over again as your guide for moving forward. Once you've achieved your first *What If?* future, do imagine another, even greater one and replicate and expand your efforts to bring that future, too, into reality.

Thought leadership has a multiplier effect. As a well-known thought leader in one niche, you will have earned a seat at the table and a role in making decisions that will have an impact far beyond your initial area of expertise. As a well-connected thought leader, you will have the right network in place to initiate far-reaching improvements in your ecosystem and well beyond. As a well-respected thought leader, you will have the platform to create and shape any *What If?* future that you can envision.

Accept, then, the opportunities presented to play on the broader stage and acknowledge your role as the leading authority, the voice of those you stand for and with. Share your expertise widely.

Thought leadership can be a lonely path. Join me in teaching others that their voice matters; show them how to get noticed, trusted, and how to gain widespread adoption for their ideas, too.

I invite you to also join the conversation online, on the Thought Leadership Lab website and social media forums. There you'll find implementation guides, videos, and other resources and you'll have a chance to share your journey with others. We have a lot to learn from each other.

In the meantime, dare to think *big*. There are so many unexplored opportunities to make a difference. There is so much work to be done to create organizations, businesses, governments, and cities that serve the needs of all. Don't let the naysayers—the ones in your head or the ones you may encounter around you—take you out of the game.

Trust that you can do this. Take one small step today and keep going. And remember to stay in service to your followers—not create a group of followers to serve you. *Thought leadership is not about being known; it is about being known for making a difference.* Keep learning and growing and regularly share what you know with others. That is the core of the thought leadership journey.

You are *ready*. Go out and change the world. Increase your impact, expand your influence, and leave a legacy that matters.

NOTES

Introduction

1. Transportation innovator Robin Chase, founder and former CEO, Zipcar; founder and CEO, Buzzcar. Visit www.robinchase.org.
2. Nina Nashif, founder and CEO, Healthbox. Visit www.healthbox.com.
3. "Ron Finley: A Guerilla Gardener in South Central LA," TED Talk, 10:46, filmed February 2013, posted March 2013, http://www.ted.com /talks/ron_finley_a_guerilla_gardener_in_south_central_la.html. Learn more about Finley at his website, http://lagreengrounds.org.
4. Katie Orenstein, founder and CEO, the OpEd Project, personal interview with author, November 5, 2012.
5. Denise Brosseau, email from Erika Brown Ekiel, February 1, 2013.
6. Springboard Enterprises, www.sb.co. By 2013, over five hundred women-led companies had gone through Springboard's accelerator programs; they have raised more than $6.2 billion in financing, have created tens of thousands of new jobs, and generate billions of dollars in annual revenues.

Getting Started

1. Kelley, T., and Littman, J., *The Ten Faces of Innovation: IDEO's Strategies for Defeating the Devil's Advocate and Driving Creativity Throughout Your Organization*, New York: Currency Doubleday, October 18, 2005.
2. GBN Podcasts, "GBN in Conversation: Andrew Blau Interviews Dan Gillmor," recorded March 23, 2011, http://www.gbn.com/mp3s/.
3. I like Springwise, www.springwise.com, or CEB Iconoculture, www.iconoculture.com.
4. Evernote, www.evernote.com.

5.   "Occam's Razor" blog by Avinash Kaushik, http://www.kaushik.net /avinash/.

6.   Avinash Kaushik, author, *Web Analytics 2.0*, personal interview with author, December 12, 2012.

7.   Transportation innovator Robin Chase, founder and former CEO, Zipcar, personal interview with author, April 12, 2012.

8.   Chase, Robin, "Fossil Fuel Is the New Slavery: Morally and Economically Corrupt," *Huffington Post*, posted October 5, 2009; retrieved April 5, 2012, from http://www.huffingtonpost.com/robin-chase/fossil-fuel-is-the-new-sl_b_310007.html.

9.   Chip Conley, founder and former CEO, Joie de Vivre Hospitality, personal interview with author, November 21, 2012.

10.   Gilmore, D., *Mediactive*, Raleigh, NC: Lulu.com, 2010. Visit www.mediactive.com.

11.   Fry, Jason, "Reinventing the Newsroom: Transparency Isn't Just for Journalists," posted January 18, 2010; retrieved April 1, 2013, from http://reinventingthenewsroom.wordpress.com/2010/01/18/transparency-isnt-just-for-journalists/.

12.   Doug Stevenson, founder and president of Story Theater International, www.storytelling-in-business.com.

13.   Lou Heckler, motivational and keynote speaker and speaker coach, www.louheckler.com.

14.   Arina Isaacson, MA, communications coaching and consulting, http://coachingforcommunicationsanfrancisco.com.

15.   KC Baker, women's thought leadership and public speaking training, www.kcbaker.com.

16.   Duarte, N., *Resonate: Present Visual Stories That Transform Audiences*, Hoboken, NJ: Wiley, 2010.

17.   Business Innovation Factory Conference, http://www.businessinnovationfactory.com.

18.   TED Talks, www.ted.com.

19.   Brené Brown, "The Power of Vulnerability," TED video, 20:20, filmed June 2010, posted December 2010, http://www.ted.com/talks/brene_brown_on_vulnerability.html.

20.   Kawasaki, G., *Enchantment: The Art of Changing Hearts, Minds and Actions*, New York: Portfolio Trade, December 31, 2012.

21.   Vanderkam, Laura, "How to Become a Guru," MoneyWatch online, posted April 1, 2013; retrieved April 2, 2013, from

http://www.cbsnews.com/8301-505125_162-57577196/how-to-become-a-guru/.

22.   Lynn Price, social entrepreneur and professional speaker, personal interview with Denise Brosseau, April 10, 2012.

23.   Penelope Trunk, http://blog.penelopetrunk.com.

Chapter 1

1.   http://www.goodreads.com/author/quotes/237609.Wilma_Mankiller.

2.   Vinod Khosla, founder, Khosla Ventures, panelist, Churchill Club event, September 13, 2012.

3.   Allen, J. S., *Bicycling Street Smarts*, Emmaus, PA: Rodale, 2001.

4.   I like http://www.springwise.com/newsletter/.

5.   Indiegogo, www.indiegogo.com, or Kickstarter, www.kickstarter.com.

6.   Schurenberg, E., "Chip Conley: The 5 Things Everyone Wants from You," *Inc. Magazine* online, posted December 12, 2011; retrieved April 1, 2013, http://www.inc.com/eric-schurenberg/chip-conley-5-things-everyone-wants.html.

Chapter 2

1.   Johnson, S., *Where Good Ideas Come From*, New York: Riverhead Trade, 2011.

2.   Johnson, S. "The Genius of the Tinkerer," *Wall Street Journal* online, posted September 25, 2010; retrieved April 1, 2013, http://online.wsj.com/article/SB10001424052748703989304575503730101860838.html.

3.   Van Ton-Quinlivan, Vice Chancellor, California Community College System, personal interviews with Denise Brosseau, 2010–2012.

4.   Wilson, E. O., *Consilience: The Unity of Knowledge*, New York: Vintage, 1999.

5.   Wolf, G., "Steve Jobs: The Next Insanely Great Thing," *Wired Magazine*, posted February 1995, retrieved April 1, 2013, http://www.wired.com/wired/archive/4.02/jobs_pr.html.

6.   Steve Craft, then Deputy Director in the Strategic Relationships Office at the NASA Langley Research Center, personal interview with author, January 16, 2012.

7.   Learn more about TED and TEDx Conferences at www.ted.com.

8.   A *skunkworks* is defined as a "a small team taken out of their normal working environment and given exceptional freedom from their organization's standard management constraints." Hindle, T., *Guide to Management Ideas and Gurus*, New York: Bloomberg Press, 2008.

9.   Caldicott, S. M., and Gelb, M. J., *Innovate Like Edison: The Five-Step System for Breakthrough Business Success*, New York: Plume, 2008.

10. Gladwell, M., *The Tipping Point: How Little Things Can Make a Big Difference*, New York: Back Bay Books, 2002.

11. Van Ton-Quinlivan, Vice Chancellor, California Community College System, personal interviews with author, 2010–2012.

12. Steve Craft, then Deputy Director in the Strategic Relationships Office at the NASA Langley Research Center, personal interview with author, January 16, 2012.

13. O'Connor, C., "SPANX Creator's Tips for Future Billionaires," posted March 2012, retrieved April 1, 2013, from http://landing.newsinc.com/forbes/video.html?vcid=23824193&free wheel=91218&sitesection=forbes.

14. "Robin Chase," YouTube video, 38:20, posted by "MIT Startup Bootcamp," October 12, 2009, http://www.youtube.com/watch?v=Ks4B82CJkpo&feature=youtube _gdata_player.

15. Sandberg, S., *Lean In: Women, Work and the Will to Lead*, New York: Knopf, 2013.

16. Savoia, A., *Pretotype It*, Amazon Digital Services, 2012.

17. VideoScribe, http://www.sparkol.com/videoscribe.php.

18. Innocentive, https://www.innocentive.com/ar/challenge/10300000035.

19. Bourin, L., "Gates Wants Geeks to Build a Better Condom," CNN, posted March 26, 2013; retrieved May 5, 2013, http://www.cnn.com/2013/03/25/health/bill-gates-condom-challenge/index.html.

20. Miki Agrawal, cofounder and owner of WILD (formerly Slice Perfect), personal interview with author, April 16, 2012.

Chapter 3

1.   Mary Hughes, political strategist, President of Hughes & Company and founder of the 2012 Project, personal interview with author, November 26, 2012.

2.   Ibid.

3.   Nina Nashif, founder and CEO, Healthbox, personal conversations with author, 2012–2013.

4.   Horan, J., and Peters, T., *The One Page Business Plan for the Creative Entrepreneur*, Oakland, CA: One Page Business Plan Company, 2004.

5.   One Page Business Plan, www.onepagebusinessplan.com.

6.   Steve Craft, then Deputy Director in the Strategic Relationships Office at the NASA Langley Research Center, personal interview with author, January 16, 2012.

Chapter 4

1.   The OpEd project runs a highly effective, experiential training program at companies, universities, and for the public at large in order to encourage more minority and women's voices into the national conversation. Katie Orenstein, CEO, the OpEd Project, personal interview with author, November 5, 2012.

2.   Commander Zoe Dunning, SC, USNR (Ret.), personal interview with author, July 8, 2011.

3.   "Derek Sivers: How to Start a Movement," TED video, 3:10, posted April 2010, downloaded April 17, 2013, http://www.ted.com/talks/derek_sivers_how_to_start_a_movement.html.

4.   Kawasaki, G., and Welch, S., *APE: Author, Publisher, Entrepreneur—How to Publish a Book*, Menlo Park, CA: Nononina Press, 2013.

5.   Guy Kawasaki interviewed by Rafe Needleman, "Guy Kawaski's Top Tips for Authors," posted by "Evernote Talks," 40:34, http://www.ustream.tv/channel/evernote-talks.

6.   Nancy Calderon, Global Lead Partner, KPMG, personal interview with author, April 18, 2012.

7.   Peter Schwartz, Senior Vice President for Global Relations and Strategic Planning for Salesforce.com, personal interview with author, December 12, 2012.

8.   Hank Leber, founder and CEO of GonnaBe, "Driving Innovation," Fast Company video, 3:18, posted at http://www.fastcompany.com/driving-innovation.

9.   Anderson, M. J., and Gilmour, N., "On Being Bold: Thought Leadership and Why It Is Risk/Reward." *The Glass Hammer*, posted August 10, 2010; retrieved April 17, 2013, http://www.theglasshammer.com/news/2010/08/10/on-being-bold-thought-leadership-is-leadership/.

10.   Transportation innovator Robin Chase, founder and former CEO, Zipcar, personal interview with author, September 1, 2010.

11.   Kathleen P. Harren, MSN MHA RN, Regional Director Nursing Institute, Providence Health & Services California, personal interview with author, January 16, 2012.

12.   Antonia Galindo, Vice President, Organizational Development, Pandora, personal conversation, December 8, 2012.

13.   Chip Conley, founder and former CEO, Joie de Vivre Hospitality, personal interview with author, November 21, 2012.

14.   Mary LoVerde, life balance expert and author, *The Invitation: When You're Ready to Take Your Next Step*, personal conversation with author, November 2012.

15.   Kathleen P. Harren, MSN MHA RN, Regional Director Nursing Institute, Providence Health & Services California, personal interview with author, January 16, 2012.

16.   Leah Busque, "The New Boom: Female Founders Rising," video highlights from the 2012 IWF World Leadership Conference, "Ideas Remaking the World," October 24–26, 2012, http://members.iwforum.org/events/past (registration required).

17.   Ali Wing, CEO and founder, giggle, personal interview with author, May 9, 2011.

18.   Todd Beauchamp, President, In2Technologies, personal conversation, June 2012.

19.   Joanna Bloor, Vice President, Advertising Operations and Sales Operations, Pandora, panel discussion, HiPower event, January 16, 2013.

20.   Bansal, S., "The Power of Failure," *New York Times* online, posted November 28, 2012; retrieved April 17, 2013, from http://opinionator.blogs.nytimes.com/2012/11/28/the-power-of-failure-2/.

21.   Beck, J., *Beck Diet Solution*, Birmingham, AL: Oxmoor House, 2007.

22.   Hill, N., and Pell, A., *Think and Grow Rich*, New York: Tarcher Books, 2005.

Chapter 5

1.   Heath, C., and Heath, D., *Switch: How to Change Things When Change Is Hard*, New York: Crown Business, 2010.

2.   Honorable Carole Beier, Kansas Supreme Court, personal interview with author, July 6, 2012.

3.   Dr. Nina Bhatti, CEO, Kokko, Inc., personal interview with author, March 25, 2012.

4.   Vocus PR-Web, "Joie de Vivre Hotels Wins Top Customer Satisfaction Ranking for 2010: Boutique Hotel Brand Ranked Best in Upper Upscale Hotel Segment," *The Street*, posted March 7, 2011; retrieved April 17, 2013, from http://www.thestreet.com/story/11049284/1/joie-de-vivre-hotels-wins-top-customer-satisfaction-ranking-for-2010-boutique-hotel-brand-ranked-best-in-upper-upscale-hotel-segment.html.

5.   Chip Conley, founder and former CEO, Joie de Vivre Hospitality, personal interview with author, November 21, 2012.

6.   Horn, S., *Pop! Create the Perfect Pitch, Title, and Tagline for Anything.* New York: Perigee Trade, 2009.

7.   Sam Horn, founder and CEO, the Intrigue Agency, personal interview with author, March 28, 2012.

8.   "Intellectual property," Merriam-Webster.com, 2013, retrieved May 12, 2013, from http://www.merriam-webster.com/dictionary/intellectual %20property.

9.   Pattison, K., "Chip Conley Took the Maslow Pyramid, Made It an Employee Pyramid and Saved His Company," *Fast Company*, posted August 25, 2010; retrieved April 17, 2013, from http://www.fastcompany.com/1685009/chip-conley-took-maslow-pyramid-made-it-employee-pyramid-and-saved-his-company.

10.   Conley, C., *Peak: How Great Companies Get Their Mojo from Maslow*, San Francisco: Jossey-Bass, 2007. This material is reproduced with permission of John Wiley & Sons, Inc.

11.   "California Community Colleges, Doing What Matters," http://doing whatmatters.cccco.edu. This material is reproduced with permission of Van Ton-Quinlivan.

12.   Alimat, Inc., www.alimat-inc.com.

13.   Creative Commons, www.creativecommons.org.

14.   Stanford Venture Lab, https://venture-lab.org/creativity.

15.   Seelig, T., *inGenius: A Crash Course on Creativity*, New York: HarperOne, 2012.

16.   Dr. Tina Seelig, Executive Director for the Stanford Technology Ventures Program, personal conversation with author, February 27, 2013.

Chapter 6

1.   Kawasaki, G., "The 120 Day Wonder: How to Evangelize a Blog," April 2006, http://blog.guykawasaki.com/2006/04/the_120_day_won.html.

2.   Avinash Kaushik, author, *Web Analytics 2.0*, personal interview with the author, December 12, 2012.

3.   Alltop, www.alltop.com.

4.   Technorati, http://technorati.com.

5.   Dr. Nina Bhatti, CEO, Kokko, Inc., personal interview with author, March 25, 2012.

6.   Peters, T., "The Brand Called You," Fast Company, posted August 31, 1997; retrieved April 17, 2013, from http://www.fastcompany.com/28905/brand-called-you.

7.   Avinash Kaushik, author, *Web Analytics 2.0*, personal interview with the author, December 12, 2012.

8.   Speaker Scott Ginsberg, http://www.hellomynameisscott.com.

9.   Tennant, D. B., "What Branding Really Means, and Why It's Usually Code for BS," April 26, 2013, http://blog.kissmetrics.com/what-branding-really-means/.

10.   Peters, T., *The Brand You 50: Fifty Ways to Transform Yourself from an "Employee" into a Brand That Shouts Distinction, Commitment, and Passion!* New York: Knopf, 1999.

11.   Schawbel, D., *Me 2.0: Build a Powerful Brand to Achieve Career Success*, New York: Kaplan, 2009.

12.   Jennifer Aaker, "Harnessing the Power of Stories," Lean In video, 19:47, April 2013, http://leanin.org/education/harnessing-the-power-of-stories/.

13.   Horn, S., "That's Intriguing #27: How to Use Stories to Make Your Business Presentations More Compelling," June 29, 2010, http://www.intrigueagency.com/thats-intriguing-27-how-to-use-stories-to-make-your-business-presentations-more-compelling/.

14.   "Sam Horn–Speaker Video," YouTube video, 8:50, posted by "The Intrigue Agency," August 7, 2012, http://www.youtube.com/watch?v=I032LimKl68.

15.   Springboard Enterprises, www.sb.co.

16.   Amy Millman, President, Springboard Enterprises, personal conversations with author, 1999–2013.

17.   Kerpen, D., *Likeable Social Media: How to Delight Your Customers, Create an Irresistible Brand, and Be Generally Amazing on Facebook (And Other Social Networks)*, New York: McGraw-Hill, 2011.

18. Saporito, M., "How to Get Noticed," "Starting with Story" blog, posted July 8, 2012; retrieved April 13, 2013, from http://startingwithstory.com/2012/07/08/how-to-get-noticed/.

19. Sanders, I., "The Right Medium Is Part of the Message," *Financial Times*, posted December 3, 2012; retrieved April 17, 2013, from http://www.ft.com/cms/s/0/4ef08202-37d5-11e2-a97e-00144feabdc0.html#axzz2Qle3m2vO.

20. Bates, Don, *Journalist Survey*, Washington, DC: George Washington University Graduate School of Political Management, 2009. http://us.cision.com/news_room/press_releases/2010/2010-1-20_gwu_survey.asp.

21. Visit our website at www.thoughtleadershiplab.com.

22. LinkedIn Influencers, http://www.linkedin.com/today/post/whoToFollow.

23. Holiday, R., *Trust Me, I'm Lying: Confessions of a Media Manipulator*, London: Portfolio Hardcover, 2012.

24. Fields, J., "Video Killed the . . . " Jonathan Fields's blog, posted February 20, 2013; retrieved April 27, 2013, from http://www.jonathanfields.com/blog/video-killed-the/.

25. Ferris, T., "How to Create a Viral Book Trailer (or Get 1,000,000 Views for Almost Anything)," Tim Ferris's blog, posted April 10, 2013; retrieved April 27, 2013, from http://www.fourhourworkweek.com/blog/2013/04/10/.

26. Aaker, J., Smith, A., Ariely, D., and Heath, C. *The Dragonfly Effect: Quick, Effective, and Powerful Ways to Use Social Media to Drive Social Change*, San Francisco: Jossey-Bass, 2010.

27. Smith, M., *The New Relationship Marketing: How to Build a Large, Loyal, Profitable Network Using the Social Web*, Hoboken, NJ: Wiley, 2011.

28. Kawasaki, G. *What the Plus!: Google+ for the Rest of Us*, New York: McGraw-Hill, 2012.

29. Avinash Kaushik's blog, http://www.kaushik.net/avinash/.

30. Market Motive, www.marketmotive.com.

31. Beth Blecherman, http://techmamas.com/bio-beth-blecherman-techmamas-com.

32. Holiday, R., *Trust Me, I'm Lying: Confessions of a Media Manipulator*, London: Portfolio Hardcover, 2012.

33. HARO: Help A Reporter Out, www.helpareporter.com.

34. Try Market Motive, http://www.marketmotive.com or look for a class at your local community college.

35. The OpEd Project, http://www.theopedproject.org.

36.   Katie Orenstein, CEO and founder, the OpEd Project, personal interview
       with author, November 5, 2012.

37.   Aaker, J., Smith, A., Ariely, D., and Heath, C. *The Dragonfly Effect:
       Quick, Effective, and Powerful Ways to Use Social Media to Drive Social
       Change*, San Francisco: Jossey-Bass, 2010.

38.   "Kevin Rose Interviews Tim Ferris," YouTube video, 54:10, posted by
       "Foundation 15," December 19, 2011,
       http://www.youtube.com/watch?v=ccFYnEGWoOc.

39.   "Oreo's Knockout Blackout Ad," *The Week*, posted February 15, 2013;
       retrieved April 17, 2013, from
       http://cdn.app.theweek.com/editions/com.dennis.theweek.issue.issue604
       /data/12604_cd018e84f42efa9d664baf
       451507fb49/web.html.

40.   Perlis, M. M., "8 Public Speaking Lessons from 57 Inaugural Speeches:
       The Good, the Bad, and the Ugly," *Forbes*, posted January 19, 2013;
       retrieved April 17, 2013, from
       http://www.forbes.com/sites/margaretperlis/2013/01/19/8-public-speaking
       -lessons-from-57-inaugural-speeches-the-good-the-bad-and-the-ugly/.

41.   Ibid.

42.   Norton, M. I., "The Ikea Effect: When Labor Leads to Love," *Harvard
       Business Review*, posted 2009; retrieved April 17, 2013, from http://hbr
       .org/web/2009/hbr-list/ikea-effect-when-labor-leads-to-love.

43.   Whatever you choose, be certain it assures subscribers of email address
       privacy and contains the ability to easily change an email address and to
       unsubscribe.

Chapter 7

1.   Peckham, M., "RIP Google Reader, Hello Four Best RSS-Reader
      Replacements," Time Tech, posted July 1, 2013; retrieved September 15,
      2013 from http://techland.time.com/2013/07/01/r-i-p-google-reader-
      hello-four-best-rss-reader-replacements/#ixzz2eyfrctlj.

2.   Griffel, M., "How We (Unexpectedly) Got 60K Users in 60 Hours,"
      Slideshare, posted October 17, 2012; retrieved September 15, 2013 from
      http://www.slideshare.net/mattangriffel/how-we-unexpectedly-got-60k-
      users-in-60-hours utm_source=slideshow&utm_medium=ssemail&utm
      _campaign=weekly_digest.

3.   Vist our website at www.thoughtleadershiplab.com.

4.   Transportation innovator Robin Chase, founder and former CEO, Zipcar,
      personal interview with author, April 9, 2012.

5.   Jerry McNellis, founder, the Compression Planning Institute, personal interview with author, December 20, 2012.

6.   The Myers & Briggs Foundation, http://www.myersbriggs.org.

7.   Levy, F., and Murnane, R. J., *The New Division of Labor: How Computers Are Creating the Next Job Market*, Princeton, NJ: Princeton University Press, 2005.

8.   The Cisco Networking Academy Program, https://www.netacad.com /web/about-us/about-networking-academy;jsessionid=7F040A5CC1246 735F7E1027A92626A22.node3.

9.   "Dennis Littky on Big Picture Ed," 2009 Pop! Tech Conference, 24:08, posted by Pop! Tech, 2009, http://poptech.org/popcasts/dennis_littky_ on_big_picture_ed.

10.   Barenblat, R., "Dennis Littky of Big Picture Learning," October 23, 2009, http://poptech.org/blog/dennis_littky_of_big_picture_learning.

11.   Michelle May, MD CSP, CEO of Am I Hungry, personal interview with author, January 4, 2013.

12.   Here's a book that will teach you how to run a great conference. Wright, D., *We've Got to START Meeting Like This*, Campbell, CA: Take Action, Inc., 2013.

13.   "Jennifer Aaker: Small Acts, Big Change," YouTube video, 1:20, posted by Stanford Business School, December 6, 2012, http://www.youtube.com/watch?v=qIX4Rp0Ab-I&list=PLxq_IXOU lvQAOwMndus4zSk86MkxsNka2.

14.   Aaker, J., Smith, A., Ariely, D., and Heath, C. *The Dragonfly Effect: Quick, Effective, and Powerful Ways to Use Social Media to Drive Social Change*, San Francisco: Jossey-Bass, 2010.

15.   Kate Purmal, business coach and strategy consultant, personal interview with author, February 1, 2013.

16.   Sandberg, S., *Lean In: Women, Work and the Will to Lead*, New York: Knopf, 2013.

17.   Lean In, www.leanin.org and Mightybell, www.mightybell.com.

18.   Michelle May, MD CSP, CEO of Am I Hungry, personal interview with author, January 4, 2013.

19.   Ellen Petry Leanse, Executive Vice President and Strategic Director, Eastwick, a tech-focused communications and PR practice, personal interview with author, December 5, 2012.

20.   Traackr, www.traackr.com.

Conclusion

1.   Quote attributed to author and poet Maya Angelou.

ACKNOWLEDGMENTS

Many wonderful people have helped me create this book, by believing it possible, cheerleading me along the way, and putting in an amazing amount of time and attention to make it a reality:

My loyal readers, who were honest and kind with their feedback: Rebecca Barfknecht, Laura Hattendorf, Hui Lancaster, Ellen Lapham, Nancy Richard Murphy, Adrienne Pierce, Erika Pretell, Laura Shact, Ellen Snee, Wako Takayama, Tricia Tong, Scott Trappe, and Debbie Wolter. A special thanks to Debbie Siegel, my cherished collaborator and friend, whose input is always invaluable. She was the one I turned to when I just could not bear to cut a chapter that desperately needed cutting, and she was always right about what to keep and what to jettison.

My magical mastermind partners, Mary LoVerde and Sam Horn, who have given me more ideas, inspiration, and acknowledgment along the way than I ever could have imagined. It was to them that I turned when I just could not get out of my own way, and they were instrumental in encouraging and pushing me forward.

My family, who supported me throughout this journey. I truly appreciate each and every one of you but most especially my mom, who was a dedicated editor of every word on every page—through dozens of different iterations—and provided much of the masterful research needed to complete this book.

My editors, including Genoveva Llosa, who "discovered" me and believed in this book right from the beginning; as well as

Clancy Drake and John Maas of Jossey-Bass, who shepherded it with great expertise along the way.

My publicists, Amy Packard of Jossey-Bass, Puja Sangar, and my longtime friend Sylvia Paull.

My clients, colleagues, and collaborators, whose success stories, advice, and bold ideas are a big part of this book: Miki Agrawal, Kare Anderson, Robbie Baxter, Todd Beauchamp, the Honorable Carole Beier, Dr. Nina Bhatti, Joanna Bloor, Nancy Calderon, Sarah Caldicott, Robin Chase, Matt Clark, Barb Coll, Chip Conley, Steve Craft, Elaine Cummings, Zoe Dunning, Erika Brown Ekiel, Antonia Galindo, Kathy Harren, Andrew Horn, Sam Horn, Mary Hughes, Avinash Kaushik, Ellen Leanse, Mary LoVerde, Alison Macondray, Dr. Michelle May, Jerry McNellis, Tom Melcher, Amy Millman, Rebecca Morgan, Nina Nashif, David Newman, Katie Orenstein, Adrian Ott, Professor Jeffrey Pfeffer, Rob Portil, Bryan Potter, Lynn Price, Kate Purmal, Jennifer Gill Roberts, Joanna Rustin, Sharon Ruwart, Peter Schwartz, Dr. Tina Seelig, Chris Shipley, Ruth Stergiou, Manisha Thakor, Lynne Twist, Ali Wing, and Dana Wright.

A very special thanks to my dear friend Van Ton-Quinlivan, whose journey from leader to thought leader was the impetus for writing this book. I have very much enjoyed our partnership and can't wait to see where it will lead next. You are an inspiration and a testament to the power of thought leadership to change the world.

ABOUT THE AUTHOR

Denise Brosseau is a well-known thought leader and subject-matter expert in entrepreneurship, women's leadership, and executive talent development. Her consultancy, the Silicon Valley–based Thought Leadership Lab, helps leaders increase their influence, expand their impact, and leave a legacy that matters. Denise's clients include executives from Apple, Roche, and SAP as well as start-up CEOs and senior leaders across multiple industries and professions.

Denise is a serial entrepreneur who founded her first company at the age of twenty-six. After a career in the technology industry, she went on to cofound two organizations that have led to over $6 billion in funding for women entrepreneurs, the Forum for Women Entrepreneurs (now Watermark) and the women's start-up launch pad Springboard Enterprises, both of which showcase and support women-led high-growth companies seeking equity capital for their businesses.

Denise has a BA from Wellesley College and an MBA from Stanford University. She is a frequent speaker at companies such as Intel, Abbott, and KPMG, as well as conferences and college campuses across the United States and internationally. In 2012, she was recognized as a Champion of Change by the White House and as one of the Top 100 Women in Northern California by the Girl

Scouts. She has appeared in the *Wall Street Journal*, *Fast Company*, *Inc. Magazine*, and on NPR. You can find her on Facebook (www .facebook.com/thoughtleadershiplab), LinkedIn (www.linkedin.com /in/denisebrosseau/), Twitter (@thoughtleadrlab, https://twitter.com /thoughtleadrlab), and at www.thoughtleadershiplab.com.

INDEX